Get Up and Go

2018

Published in Ireland by
GET UP AND GO PUBLICATIONS LTD
Camboline, Hazelwood, Sligo, F91 NP04, Ireland.
Email: info@getupandgodiary.com
www.getupandgodiary.com

Compiled by Eileen Forrestal
Graphic design by Nuala Redmond
Illustrations: Sophia Murray; dreamstime.com; shutterstock.com
Printed in Ireland by GPS Colour Graphics.

Copyright c 2007-2018 Get Up And Go Publications Ltd.

All right reserved. No part of this publication may be reproduced, stored in, or introduced into, a retrieval system, or transmitted in any form, or by any means (electronic, mechanical, scanning, recording or otherwise) without the prior permission of the Publisher. Any person who does any unauthorised act in relation to this publication may be liable to criminal prosecution and civil claim for damages.

2018 BANK AND PUBLIC HOLIDAYS

REPUBLIC OF IRELAND
New Year's Day, 1 January;
St Patrick's Day Bank Holiday, 19 March;
Good Friday, 30 March;
Easter Monday, 2 April;
May Day Bank Holiday, 7 May;
June Bank Holiday, 4 June;
August Bank Holiday, 6 August;
October Bank Holiday, 29 October;
Christmas Day, 25 December;
St Stephen's Day, 26 December.

NORTHERN IRELAND
New Year's Day, 1 January;
Good Friday, 30 March;
May Day Holiday, 7 May;
Orangemen's Holiday, 12 July;
Christmas Day, 25 December;
St Patrick's Day, 19 March;
Easter Monday, 2 April;
Spring Bank Holiday, 28 May;
Summer Bank Holiday, 27 August;
Boxing Day, 26 December.

ENGLAND, SCOTLAND AND WALES
New Year's Day, 1 January;
Easter Monday, 2 April;
Spring Bank Holiday, 28 May;
Christmas Day, 25 December;
Good Friday, 30 March;
May Day Holiday, 7 May;
Summer Bank Holiday, 27 August;
Boxing Day, 26 December.

UNITED STATES OF AMERICA
New Year's Day, 1 January;
Presidents' Day, 19 February;
Independence Day, 4 July;
Columbus Day, 8 October;
Thanksgiving Day, 22 November;
Martin Luther King Day, 15 January;
Memorial Day, 28 May;
Labour Day, 3 September;
Veterans Day, 11 November;
Christmas Day, 25 December.

CANADA
New Year's Day, 1 January;
Heritage Day, 19 February;
St Patrick's Day, 19 March;
Easter Monday, 2 April;
Canada Day, 1 July;
Thanksgiving Day, 8 October;
Christmas Day, 25 December;
Family Day, 19 February;
Commonwealth Day, 12 March;
Good Friday, 30 March;
Victoria Day 21 May;
Labour Day, 3 September;
Rememberance Day, 11 November;
Boxing Day, 26 December.

AUSTRALIA (NATIONAL HOLIDAYS)
New Year's Day, 1 January;
Good Friday, 30 March;
Anzac Day 25 April;
Christmas Day, 25 December;
Australia Day, 26 January;
Easter Monday, 2 April;
Queen's Birthday, 1 October;
Boxing Day, 26 December.

2018 CALENDAR

JANUARY
Mon	Tue	Wed	Thu	Fri	Sat	Sun
1	2	3	4	5	6	7
8	9	10	11	12	13	14
15	16	17	18	19	20	21
22	23	24	25	26	27	28
29	30	31				

FEBRUARY
Mon	Tue	Wed	Thu	Fri	Sat	Sun
			1	2	3	4
5	6	7	8	9	10	11
12	13	14	15	16	17	18
19	20	21	22	23	24	25
26	27	28				

MARCH
Mon	Tue	Wed	Thu	Fri	Sat	Sun
			1	2	3	4
5	6	7	8	9	10	11
12	13	14	15	16	17	18
19	20	21	22	23	24	25
26	27	28	29	30	31	

APRIL
Mon	Tue	Wed	Thu	Fri	Sat	Sun
						1
2	3	4	5	6	7	8
9	10	11	12	13	14	15
16	17	18	19	20	21	22
23	24	25	26	27	28	29
30						

MAY
Mon	Tue	Wed	Thu	Fri	Sat	Sun
	1	2	3	4	5	6
7	8	9	10	11	12	13
14	15	16	17	18	19	20
21	22	23	24	25	26	27
28	29	30	31			

JUNE
Mon	Tue	Wed	Thu	Fri	Sat	Sun
				1	2	3
4	5	6	7	8	9	10
11	12	13	14	15	16	17
18	19	20	21	22	23	24
25	26	27	28	29	30	

JULY
Mon	Tue	Wed	Thu	Fri	Sat	Sun
						1
2	3	4	5	6	7	8
9	10	11	12	13	14	15
16	17	18	19	20	21	22
23	24	25	26	27	28	29
30	31					

AUGUST
Mon	Tue	Wed	Thu	Fri	Sat	Sun
		1	2	3	4	5
6	7	8	9	10	11	12
13	14	15	16	17	18	19
20	21	22	23	24	25	26
27	28	29	30	31		

SEPTEMBER
Mon	Tue	Wed	Thu	Fri	Sat	Sun
					1	2
3	4	5	6	7	8	9
10	11	12	13	14	15	16
17	18	19	20	21	22	23
24	25	26	27	28	29	30

OCTOBER
Mon	Tue	Wed	Thu	Fri	Sat	Sun
1	2	3	4	5	6	7
8	9	10	11	12	13	14
15	16	17	18	19	20	21
22	23	24	25	26	27	28
29	30	31				

NOVEMBER
Mon	Tue	Wed	Thu	Fri	Sat	Sun
			1	2	3	4
5	6	7	8	9	10	11
12	13	14	15	16	17	18
19	20	21	22	23	24	25
26	27	28	29	30		

DECEMBER
Mon	Tue	Wed	Thu	Fri	Sat	Sun
					1	2
3	4	5	6	7	8	9
10	11	12	13	14	15	16
17	18	19	20	21	22	23
24	25	26	27	28	29	30
31						

Dear Reader,

We are delighted that you are holding this Get Up and Go Diary for Busy Women 2018 in your hand today. You are about to embark on a wonderful journey with 'the world's best loved transformational diary'.

Whether you have chosen this diary for yourself or received it as a gift from a friend, we know it will provide the inspiration, encouragement, motivation and empowerment you need as you progress towards fulfilling your goals and dreams in 2018.

If you would like to connect with our growing Get Up and Go community, we invite you to visit our website **www.getupandgodiary.com** where you can follow our blog, find out about our new products, plus details of special offers and upcoming Get Up and Go events.

You may also like to follow us on Facebook, Twitter or Instagram for additional words of inspiration and encouragement.

Whether this is your first Get Up and Go Diary or you are a regular and loyal customer we thank you and trust that you will benefit from the words of wisdom contained therein. We would love you to share the value of the Get Up and Go Diaries with your family and friends.

Best wishes for the year ahead!

Sincerely,

Eileen, Brendan, and the Get Up and Go team

This diary belongs to: _____

_____

Address: _____

_____

Tel: _____ Email: _____

EMERGENCY NUMBERS

_____

_____

BUCKET LIST
FOR *January*

> Open different doors, you may find a you there that you never knew was yours. Anything can happen.
>
> Mary Poppins

Take time out for you.

January

Tell me, what is it you plan to do with your one wild and precious life?
— Mary Oliver

Listen to your heart

The most effective way to do it, is to do it.
— Amelia Earhart

No one else can dance your dance.
No one else can sing your song.
No one else can write your story.
— Lisa Nichols

My destination is no longer a place, rather a new way of seeing.
— Marcel Proust

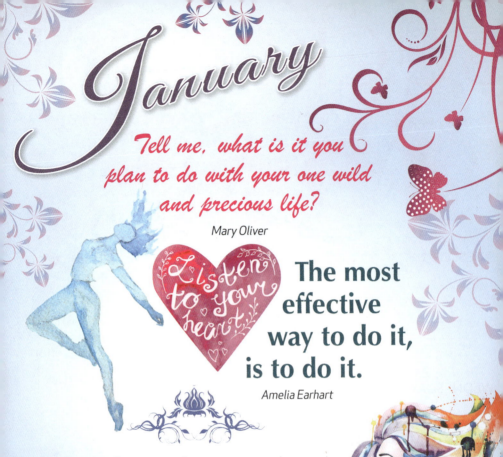

MONDAY 1
HAPPY NEW YEAR!

Get up and Go for 2018

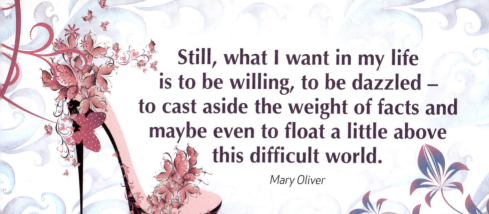

> Still, what I want in my life is to be willing, to be dazzled – to cast aside the weight of facts and maybe even to float a little above this difficult world.
>
> *Mary Oliver*

TUESDAY 2

Significant personal achievements require effort

WEDNESDAY 3

Try beginners luck again

THURSDAY 4

Challenges always test our resolve

FRIDAY 5

Sometimes the hardest thing to do is let go what you are holding on to

January

Live with no time out.

Simone de Beauvoir

YOU WILL NEVER BE OLD

You will never be old
With a twinkle in your eye,
With the Springtime in your heart
As you watch the Winter fly.
You will never be old
While you have a smile to share,
While you wonder at mankind
And you find the time to care,
While there's magic in your world
And a special dream to hold,
While you still can laugh at life,
You never will be old.

Iris Hesselden

FOLLOW YOUR HEART AND DREAM

SATURDAY 6

Let yourself wonder

SUNDAY 7

Your life is all up (and down) to you

ABOUT CHILDREN

Your children are not your children. They are the sons and daughters of life's longing for itself. They come through you but not from you. And though they are with you, they belong not to you. You may give them your love but not your thoughts, for they have their own thoughts. You may house their bodies but not their souls, for their souls dwell in the house of tomorrow, which you cannot visit, not even in your dreams. You may strive to be like them, but seek not to make them like you. For life goes not backward nor tarries with yesterday. You are the bows from which your children as living arrows are sent forth. The archer sees the mark upon the path of the infinite. And he bends you with his might that his arrows may go swift and far. Let your bending in the archer's hands be for happiness; for even as he loves the arrow that flies, so he loves the bow that is stable.

Khalil Gibran

We are born at a given moment, in a given place and, like vintage years of wine, we have the qualities of the year and of the season of which we are born.
Carl Jung

Feminism isn't about making women stronger. Women are already strong. It's about changing the way the world perceives that strength.
GD Anderson

Friends are angels who lift our feet when our own wings have trouble remembering how to fly.

January

MONDAY 8

There is wisdom in nature – observe it

TUESDAY 9

Do it now – there is no 'later'

"Where are you going?"
"I don't know."
"Then stay put, sit still, and think.
The real journey is within."

Rice bowl
FROM MAMA RAE

INGREDIENTS
½ cup brown rice
½ cup wild rice
2 spring onion
2 cloves garlic
3 teaspoons garam masala
1 can of coconut milk
1 red capsicum
1 small courgette
250gm mushrooms
2 limes
1 cup chopped coriander

THE HOW-TO PART:
Rinse and cook the rice separately (brown rice for 25 minutes, 30 for wild rice). Sauté the spring onions and garlic for 5 minutes, add the garam masala. Stir to mix well and add the coconut milk and red capsicum, courgette and mushrooms (sliced), stir until cooked. Add the rices and juice of the limes, and heat. Just before serving add the coriander.

MAMA RAE'S INSIDE SECRETS
Add 1 cup of snow peas for a splash of green. Lemon juice works as well as lime. You can add parsley instead of coriander.

WEDNESDAY 10

You're never too old to be young.
Snow White

Don't give up on your dreams

THURSDAY 11

Speak kindly to yourself about yourself

FRIDAY 12

Avoid gossip

SATURDAY 13

Enjoy a complaint free day

SUNDAY 14

Organise a reunion of old friends

January

MONDAY 15

Remember everything has a funny side

TUESDAY 16

Bad money habits are serious

10 POWERFUL AFFIRMATIONS
I am unique and valuable.
I let go of the hurts of the past and forgive myself and others.
I change all thoughts of harm to thoughts of healing.
I accept myself and others as we are now.
I am grateful for all my blessings.
I am willing to give up all thoughts and feelings of not being good enough.
I am beautiful and loving.
I know I deserve, and can achieve, my dreams.
I trust in the process of life.
I am safe and supported in the universe.

WEDNESDAY 17

With rights come responsibilities

I would maintain that thanks are the highest form of thought; and that gratitude is happiness doubled by wonder.

GK Chesterton

Live so that when your children think of fairness and integrity, they think of you.

H Jackson Brown, Jr

THURSDAY **18**

Have a bath by candlelight

FRIDAY **19**

Regularly do whatever nourishes your soul

SATURDAY **20**

Spend time with happy people

SUNDAY **21**

Let go of what no longer serves you

January

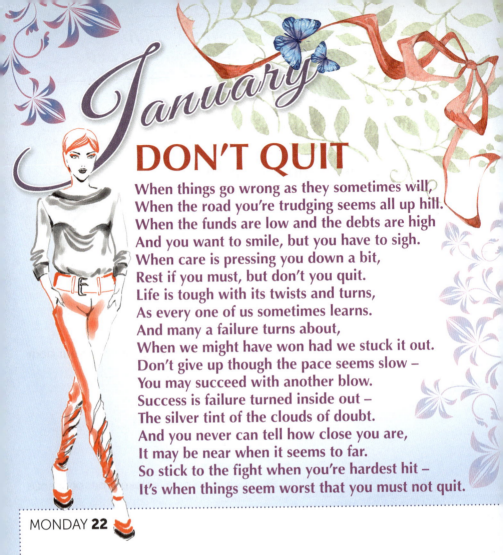

DON'T QUIT

When things go wrong as they sometimes will,
When the road you're trudging seems all up hill.
When the funds are low and the debts are high
And you want to smile, but you have to sigh.
When care is pressing you down a bit,
Rest if you must, but don't you quit.
Life is tough with its twists and turns,
As every one of us sometimes learns.
And many a failure turns about,
When we might have won had we stuck it out.
Don't give up though the pace seems slow –
You may succeed with another blow.
Success is failure turned inside out –
The silver tint of the clouds of doubt.
And you never can tell how close you are,
It may be near when it seems to far.
So stick to the fight when you're hardest hit –
It's when things seem worst that you must not quit.

MONDAY 22

Use your passion to inspire your purpose

TUESDAY 23

Don't hold grudges

> *The best and most beautiful things in the world cannot be seen or even touched – they must be felt with the heart.*

WEDNESDAY 24

Avoid taking things personally – it's disempowering

THURSDAY 25

You must rest your mind as well as your body

FRIDAY 26

Make time for silence

SATURDAY 27

Do not be afraid to ask questions

SUNDAY 28

Self care is not an optional extra

MONDAY 29

Get sufficient exercise

TUESDAY 30

Be kind and generous – for goodness sake

WEDNESDAY 31

Apologise from your heart not your lips

KIDS WHO ARE DIFFERENT

Here's to the kids who are different,
The kids who don't always get 'A's,
The kids who have ears twice the size of their peers,
And noses that go on for days...
Here's to the kids who are different,
The kids they call crazy or dumb,
The ones that don't fit, with the guts and the grit,
Who dance to a different drum...
Here's to the kids who are different,
The kids with the mischievous streak,
For when they are grown, as history's shown,
It's their difference that makes them unique.

Author unknown

> *I would like to be known as an intelligent woman, a courageous woman, a loving woman, a woman who teaches by being.*
> — Maya Angelou

BUCKET LIST
FOR *February*

Always remember that you are absolutely unique. Just like everyone else.
— Margaret Mead

THURSDAY 1

Let yourself be pulled towards new adventures

Dear Woman,

**Sometimes
you'll be just too much woman –
too smart,
too beautiful,
too strong,
too much of something
that makes a man feel like less of a man,
which will start making you feel
like you have to be less of a woman.
The biggest mistake you can make
is removing jewels from your crown
to make it easier for a man to carry.
When this happens,
I need you to understand
you do not need a smaller crown.
You need a man with bigger hands.**

Michael Reid

The older we get, the fewer things seem worth waiting in line for.

February

SIX BEST DOCTORS IN THE WORLD:
1. Sunlight
2. Rest
3. Exercise
4. Diet
5. Water
6. Friendship

JUST A MOMENT!

Can you spare a moment
Throughout a busy day,
To chat to someone lonely
You meet upon your way?
So many folk are lonely,
And need a little care,
A word or two of comfort,
You could so easily spare.
And by your understanding,
The little things you've done,
You'll make the day much brighter,
And a far less lonely one.

FRIDAY 2

Life is not fair. If we want a fair world, it's up to us to be fair

SATURDAY 3

Be willing to forgive

SUNDAY 4

Trust yourself to know who to trust

GROWING OLD

Lord, Thou knowest better than I know myself
that I am growing old, and will someday be old.
Keep me from the fatal habit of thinking I must say
something on every subject, and on every occasion.
Release me from craving to straighten out everybody's affairs;
Make me thoughtful, but not moody, helpful but not bossy.
With my vast store of wisdom, it seems a pity not to use it all –
But thou knowest lord that I still want a few friends at the end!
Keep my mind free from the recital of endless detail –
give me wings to get to the point.
Seal my lips on aches and pains; they are increasing, and love
of rehearsing them is becoming sweeter as the years go by.
I dare not ask for grace enough to enjoy the tales of others'
pains, but help me to endure them with patience.
I dare not ask for improved memory, but for growing humility
and a lessening cocksureness when my memory seems to
clash with the memories of others.
Teach me that glorious lesson that occasionally I may be mistaken
Keep me reasonably sweet.
I want to be a saint, but not one who is hard
to live with – for a sour old person is one
the of crowning works of the Devil.
Give me the ability to see good things in unexpected
places, and talents in unexpected people, and
please give me the grace to tell them so!!

Margot Benary-Isbert

*Follow what you are genuinely
passionate about and let
that guide you to your
destination.*

Diane Sawyer

February

DO MORE
Do more than exist; Live.
Do more than touch; Feel.
Do more than look; Observe.
Do more than hear; Listen.
Do more than listen; Understand.
Do more than think; Reflect.
Do more than talk; Say something.

A year from now, you will wish you had started today.

MONDAY 5

Getting your own way isn't always winning

TUESDAY 6

Don't indulge in gossip

WEDNESDAY 7

Quit looking back, you're not going that way

We don't grow older, we grow riper.
— Pablo Picasso

February

THURSDAY 8

The only time you have is now

FRIDAY 9

Learn what there is to learn and move on

SATURDAY 10

Make amends

**It was only a sunny smile
And little it cost in the giving.
But like morning light,
It scattered the night
And made the day worth living.**
F Scott Fitzgerald

SUNDAY 11

Procrastination is the thief of time

Procrastination is the art of keeping up with yesterday.

MONDAY 12

Turn off the noise and be with life

TUESDAY 13

Be secure in your values

Self care is not selfish or self indulgent. We cannot nurture others from a dry well. We need to take care of our own needs first, only then we can give from our surplus, our abundance, and not resent it being taken from us.

By realising our own self we become full, with nothing more to gain in life. Life becomes perfect.

WEDNESDAY 14
St Valentine's Day

Mind your own business

THURSDAY 15

Take time out to play

February

FRIDAY 16

Plan a girls' night out

SATURDAY 17

Find something productive to do with your hands

SUNDAY 18

Everything is negotiable

Irresistible blueberry muffins
FROM MAMA RAE

INGREDIENTS
2 cups gluten free flour
1 tablespoon baking powder
½ teaspoon salt
¼ cup coconut oil – melted
½ cup apple sauce
½ cup almond milk
½ cup maple syrup or coconut sugar
1 teaspoon vanilla
2 cups frozen blueberries

THE HOW-TO PART
1. Turn oven on to 180 degrees.
2. Grease your muffin tins or prepare patty pans on a tray.
3. Sift the flour, salt and baking powder into a bowl. Add the coconut sugar if you are using it.
4. Into another bowl put the apple sauce, maple syrup (if using), milk, vanilla, coconut oil and apple sauce. Mix.
5. Pour the wet ingredients into the flour and gently stir until almost mixed through.
6. Finally, gently mix the blueberries through.
7. Put tablespoons of the mix into prepared muffin tray/patty pans and bake for 30 to 35 minutes.

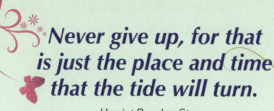

Never give up, for that is just the place and time that the tide will turn.

Harriet Beecher Stowe

MONDAY 19

Learn to accept 'no' for an answer

TUESDAY 20

Communicate clearly; people do not know what your are thinking

WEDNESDAY 21

Read something new

THURSDAY 22

Just make a start

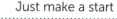

One friend with whom you have a lot in common is better than three with whom you struggle to find things to talk about.

Today charting your own course isn't just more necessary than ever before, it's also much easier, and much more fun.

Pink

FRIDAY 23

Treat others the way you want others to treat you

SATURDAY 24

Let your heart speak

SUNDAY 25

Give up any destructive habits

10 SIMPLE HEALTH TIPS FOR BUSY WOMEN

1. Don't skip breakfast.
2. Snack on fruit and nuts.
3. Eat regular meals.
4. Don't buy foods you know you shouldn't be eating.
5. Exercise.
6. Stay hydrated.
7. Get enough sleep.
8. Relax.
9. Find some time for yourself.
10. Be positive.

February

When we do the best that we can, we never know what miracle is wrought in our life, or in the life of another.

To laugh often and much.
To win the respect of intelligent people,
and the affection of children.
To earn the appreciation of honest critics.
To apreciate beauty.
To find the best in others.
To leave the world a bit better, whether by a healthy child,
or a garden patch.
To know even one life has breathed easier because you have lived.
This is to have succeeded.

MONDAY 26

Design a vision board and 'see' your future

TUESDAY 27

Figure out what your gifts are and use them

WEDNESDAY 28

Be the person you want to be

BUCKET LIST FOR *March*

_____
_____
_____
_____
_____
_____
_____
_____

*The best things in life are free.
The second best are very expensive.*

Coco Chanel

When connections are real, they simply never die. They can be buried or ignored or walked away from, but never broken. If you have deeply resonated with another person or place, the connection remains despite any distance, time, situation, lack of presence, or circumstance. If you're doubtful then just try it – go and revisit a person or place and see if there is any sense at all of the space between then and now. If it was truly real, you will be instantly swept back into the moment it was before it left – to the same year and place with the same wonder and hope, comfort and heartbeat. Real connections live on forever.

Victoria Erickson

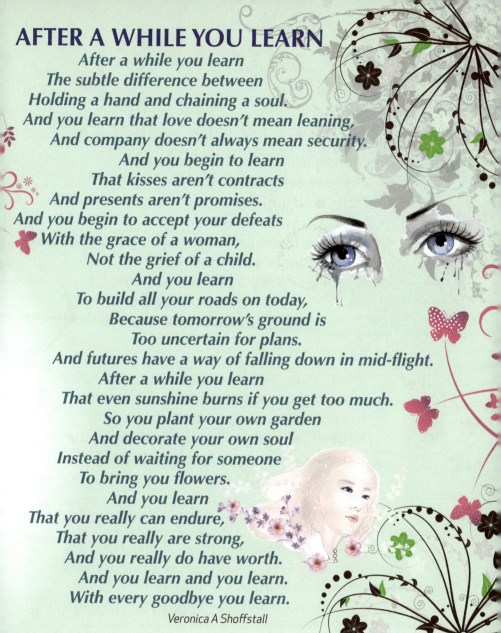

AFTER A WHILE YOU LEARN

After a while you learn
The subtle difference between
Holding a hand and chaining a soul.
And you learn that love doesn't mean leaning,
And company doesn't always mean security.
And you begin to learn
That kisses aren't contracts
And presents aren't promises.
And you begin to accept your defeats
With the grace of a woman,
Not the grief of a child.
And you learn
To build all your roads on today,
Because tomorrow's ground is
Too uncertain for plans.
And futures have a way of falling down in mid-flight.
After a while you learn
That even sunshine burns if you get too much.
So you plant your own garden
And decorate your own soul
Instead of waiting for someone
To bring you flowers.
And you learn
That you really can endure,
That you really are strong,
And you really do have worth.
And you learn and you learn.
With every goodbye you learn.

Veronica A Shoffstall

THURSDAY 1

Take a walk outdoors, sit and enjoy nature

March

HOW TO BE MORE CONFIDENT

Don't compare yourself with others.
Prepare for the occasion.
Dress to impress.
Relax. Go with the flow.
Trust yourself, you are more capable than you think.
Ignore your inner critic – it lies!
Keep a positive attitude.
Be interested in others.
Smile. Love what you do.

What you have learned from experience is worth much more than gold. If you have a house, it may burn down. Any kind of possession can be lost, but your experience is yours forever. Keep it and find a way to use it.

FRIDAY 2

Be wise about your plans for the future

SATURDAY 3

Accept yourself and all that you are

My advice: don't waste so much time worrying about your skin or your weight. Develop what you do — what you put your hands on in the world.

Meryl Streep

I AM THERE

Look for me when the tide is high
And the gulls are wheeling overhead
When the autumn wind sweeps the cloudy sky
And one by one the leaves are shed
Look for me when the trees are bare
And the stars are bright in the frosty sky
When the morning mist hangs on the air
And shorter darker days pass by.
I am there, where the river flows
And salmon leap to a silver moon
Where the insects hum and the tall grass grows
And sunlight warms the afternoon
I am there in the busy street
I take your hand in the city square
In the market place where the people meet
In your quiet room – I am there
I am the love you cannot see
And all I ask is – look for me.

       Iris Hesselden

SUNDAY **4**

You are unique and valuable

> Most of us have trouble juggling. The woman who says she doesn't is someone whom I admire, but have never met.
> *Barbara Walters*

MONDAY 5

Listen to music

> *Change is possible and following your heart is not an abstraction, but rather the key to good leadership.*
> *Charlotte Bunch*

TUESDAY 6

Be a role model for others

WEDNESDAY 7

Deal with any outstanding issues

THURSDAY 8

Think kind thoughts

March

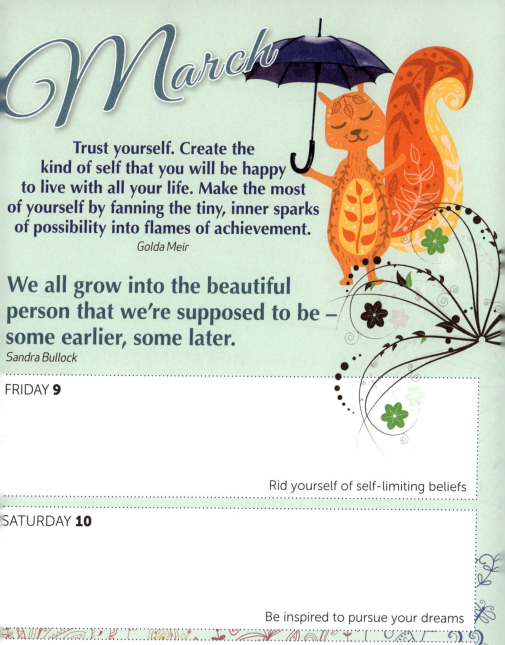

Trust yourself. Create the kind of self that you will be happy to live with all your life. Make the most of yourself by fanning the tiny, inner sparks of possibility into flames of achievement.
Golda Meir

We all grow into the beautiful person that we're supposed to be – some earlier, some later.
Sandra Bullock

FRIDAY 9

Rid yourself of self-limiting beliefs

SATURDAY 10

Be inspired to pursue your dreams

SUNDAY 11
Mother's Day

Engage in meaningful activities

March

Parents can only give good advice or put their children on the right path, but the final forming of a persons character lies in their own hands.
Anne Frank

MONDAY 12

Dance to the beat of your own drum

10 SIMPLE TIME SAVING TIPS
1. Plan ahead.
2. Freeze emergency meals.
3. Two words – slow cooker!
4. Delegate .
5. Wake up a little bit earlier.
6. Get ready for the morning the night before.
7. Set up a car pool.
8. Pay bills by direct debit.
9. Squeeze in some exercise at random moments.
10. Learn to say no!

Failing is not a crime. What is important is that if you fail at something, you do not make yourself a failure. You pick yourself up, you dust yourself of and you try again, using the lessons you have learned.

TUESDAY 13

Listen to your children

Don't worry if people think you're crazy. Be crazy. Have that kind of intoxicating insanity that lets other people dream outside of the lines and become who they're destined to be.

WEDNESDAY 14

Imagine it possible first

THURSDAY 15

The enemy of creativity is self-doubt

FRIDAY 16

Be enthusiastic

Simple spicy egg dish
FROM MAMA RAE

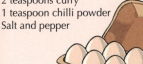

INGREDIENTS
12 hard-boiled eggs
1 onion
2 x 425gm cans diced tomatoes
2 teaspoons curry
1 teaspoon chilli powder
Salt and pepper

THE HOW-TO PART
Saute the onion in two tablespoons of water for 5 minutes on medium heat. Stir in the curry powder and add the tomatoes, stirring to mix everything. Add salt and pepper to taste. Serve with the boiled eggs cut in halves.

MAMA RAE'S INSIDE SECRETS
You can add almost anything to this recipe, celery, mushrooms, capsicums, peas, spinach. Add chopped herbs like parsley, coriander and basil. Instead of the curry try an Italian or Moroccan herb mix

March

SATURDAY 17
Happy St. Patricks Day

Allow yourself to daydream

I think that you find your own way. You have your own rules. You have your own understanding of yourself, and that's what yore going to count on. In the end it's what feels right to you. Not what your mother told you, not what some actress told you, not what anybody else told you, but the still small voice that you have discovered for yourself.

Meryl Streep

Strawberry smoothie

2 cups frozen unsweetened strawberries
½ cup cranberry/raspberry juice
¼ cup orange juice
½ cup vanilla yogurt
2 fresh strawberries for garnish (optional)
Place the strawberries in the bottom of a blender
or food processor fitted with a metal blade.
Add the juices.
Top with the yogurt and puree until smooth.
Pour into glasses and garnish with each with a strawberry.
Serve immediately.

SUNDAY 18

Acknowledge those who support you

> *I love deadlines.*
> *I like the whooshing sound they*
> *make as they fly by.*
>
> Douglas Adams

MONDAY **19**

Get enough sleep

TUESDAY **20**

Do not compare yourself to others

WEDNESDAY **21**

Don't just chat, connect

THURSDAY **22**

Believe anything is possible

FRIDAY **23**

Have a bath by candlelight

March

WHOSE CHILD IS THIS?

"Whose child is this?" I asked one day
Seeing a little one out at play
"Mine", said the parent with a tender smile
"Mine to keep a little while
To bathe her hands and comb her hair
To tell her what she is to wear
To prepare her that she may always be good
And each day do the things she should"
"Whose child is this?" I asked again
As the door opened and someone came in
"Mine", said the teacher with the same tender smile
"Mine, to keep just for a little while
To teach her how to be gentle and kind
To train and direct her dear little mind
To help her live by every rule
And get the best she can from school"
"Whose child is this?" I ask once more
Just as the little one entered the door
"Ours" said the parent and the teacher as they smiled
And each took the hand of the little child
"Ours to love and train together
Ours this blessed task forever."

Author unknown

SATURDAY 24

Encourage others

SUNDAY 25

Become more spontaneous, try out new things

One's life has value so long as one attributes value to the lives of others, by means of love, friendship, and compassion.

Simone de Beauvoir

Love yourself first and everything else falls into line. You really have to love yourself to get anything done in this world.

Lucille Ball

Let's have some SPRING tea!

MONDAY 26

Don't buy the lie

TUESDAY 27

Brainstorm with your friends and family

WEDNESDAY 28

Keep a journal

Have the courage to accept that you're not perfect — nothing is and no one is — and that's okay.
— Katie Couric

Dance is the hidden language of the soul

I'm sorry — If you were right, I'd agree with you.
— Robin Williams

THURSDAY 29

Crystallise your desires into words and deeds

FRIDAY 30
Good Friday

Honour your word

SATURDAY 31

You can leave the past behind

BUCKET LIST
FOR *April*

> **Even the most beautiful of the stars are taken for granted night after night.**

SUNDAY 1
Easter Sunday

Have a laugh with your friends

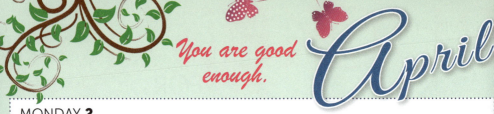

You are good enough.

April

MONDAY 2
Bank holiday

Find someone to hug, and hug them

TUESDAY 3

Decide what is important to you

WEDNESDAY 4

Do what needs to be done

THURSDAY 5

Don't take anything, or anyone, for granted

FRIDAY 6

Stuff happens

SATURDAY 7

Imagine life from another's perspective

SUNDAY 8

Contribute to a better way

Take control of your life. Taking full responsibility for the things that happen to you gives you power. Find an activity that makes you happy and practice it. Limit bad habits, cultivate good ones. Don't procrastinate. Your life will be shaped by the choices and decisions you make. Own them.

I am only one, but still I am one. I cannot do everything, but still I can do something; and because I cannot do everything, I will not refuse to do something that I can do.

Helen Keller

Life teaches us how to live it, if we live long enough.

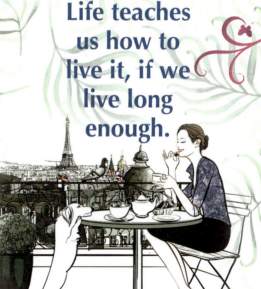

What material success does is provide you with the ability to concentrate on other things that matter, such as being able to make a difference, not only in your own life, but in other peoples' lives.
Oprah Winfrey

How you see where you are depends on where you have been.

MONDAY 9

Resist the lure of glossy advertising

TUESDAY 10

Learn from your mistakes

WEDNESDAY 11

Random complaining is unproductive

THURSDAY 12

Have a daily to-do list

FRIDAY 13

You can't please everyone

SATURDAY 14

Empower children to be responsible adults

SUNDAY 15

Compliment when a compliment is due

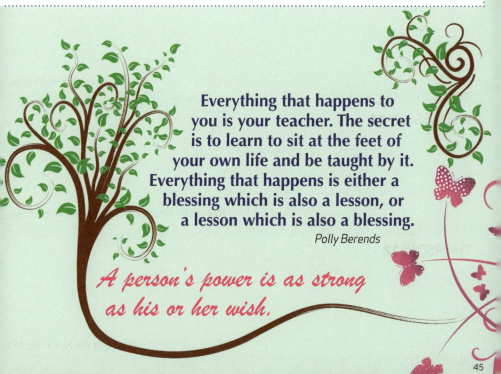

Everything that happens to you is your teacher. The secret is to learn to sit at the feet of your own life and be taught by it. Everything that happens is either a blessing which is also a lesson, or a lesson which is also a blessing.
Polly Berends

A person's power is as strong as his or her wish.

April

Courage doesn't always roar. Sometimes courage is the little voice a the end of the day that says 'I'll try again tomorrow'.

Mary Anne Radmacher

MONDAY 16

Aspire to excellence

TUESDAY 17

You can always find something positive to say

WEDNESDAY 18

To get unstuck, do something, anything!

THURSDAY 19

Make an intentional effort to slow down

What counts is not the length of life but how it is lived. If a person performs good deeds and helps others, it is a life full of merit.

Cheng Yen

For beautiful eyes, look for the good in others; for beautiful lips, speak only words of kindness; and for poise, walk with the knowledge that you are never alone.

Audrey Hepburn

FRIDAY 20

Honour your parents

SATURDAY 21

Get interested in other people

SUNDAY 22

Ask for advice and listen to it

Almond bread

FROM MAMA RAE

INGREDIENTS
2 cups almond meal
$3/4$ cup arrowroot flour
2 tablespoons flax meal
1 tablespoon chia seeds
1 teaspoon baking soda
A pinch of salt
3 eggs
¼ pint milk
¼ pint coconut oil
2 teaspoons maple syrup
1 tablespoon apple cider vinegar

THE HOW-TO PART
In one bowl mix the almond meal, arrowroot flour, flax meal, chia seeds, baking soda and salt.
In another bowl beat the eggs, milk, coconut oil, maple syrup and apple cider vinegar. Stir the egg mix into the flour. Pour into a loaf tin and bake for 30-40 minutes at 18°.

MAMA RAE'S INSIDE SECRETS
Adding herbs of your choice changes the taste of the bread.

People make their own luck by daring to follow their instincts, taking risks, and embracing every possibility.

Estée Lauder

MONDAY 23

Welcome the perspective of others

TUESDAY 24

Don't overthink it

WEDNESDAY 25

When you mess up, 'fess up

April

As hard as it is, and as tired as I am, I force myself to get dinner at least once a week with my girlfriends, or have a sleepover. Otherwise my life is just work.
Jennifer Laurence.

THURSDAY **26**

Everyone has hidden struggles

FRIDAY **27**

Eat well, your body will thank you

SATURDAY **28**

Be ok with imperfections

SUNDAY **29**

Celebrate all that is good in your life

April

I think best in a hot bath, with my head tilted back and my feet up high.
Elizabeth Jane Howard

MONDAY 30

If you are overburdened, delegate!

Energy bites

INGREDIENTS
3.5oz pecans
2.6oz raisins
1tbsp ground flax seed
1tbsp cocoa powder
1tbsp syrup
1.7oz desiccated coconut
2tbsp peanut butter

METHOD
Put pecans in a food processor and blitz to crumbs. Add raisins, peanut butter, flax seed, cocoa powder and syrup, then pulse to combine.

Shape mixture into golf-ball sized balls and roll in desiccated coconut to coat. Put in fridge to firm for 20 minutes.

Food safety tips

Good practices in the kitchen will save you and your family from food poisoning. Sometimes we can get over-sensitive to home food hygiene and we see mothers all the time, spraying what are effectively chemicals on kitchen surfaces where it can get into the food. What effect will this have we wonder? Ironically if you don't get exposed to bacteria or germs, your immune system doesn't know how to fight them when you meet it outside the home. However, you need to operate a good clean system when you are dealing with different types of food so you can stay healthy without the over-use of chemicals. Here are the key points to remember:

- Wash and dry your hands well before and after handling food.
- All meat, poultry and eggs should be cooked through to kill any bacteria.
- If you are cooking a chicken, don't wash it as you may spread bacteria – the heat will kill everything when you cook it.
- Don't use the same utensils and surfaces to cut or prepare raw meat and vegetables. Change the knife!
- Clean counters and boards well with anti-bacterial cleaner or put them in the dishwasher after they have been in contact with raw meat. Never cut something else on a board that you have been using to cut raw meat or poultry.
- Wash fruits and vegetables under running tap water and scrub well to remove pesticides and any bacteria. Don't leave produce at room temperature for long periods as bacteria can flourish.
- If you have leftovers, cool them completely, then cover well and store in the fridge. If the food has been lying around in kitchen heat for a long time, throw it away, don't put it in the fridge. You will be storing up trouble.

BUCKET LIST FOR May

TUESDAY 1

Give credit where credit is due

WEDNESDAY 2

Keep your thoughts to yourself

May

There's one sad truth in life I've found
While journeying east and west –
The only folks we really wound
Are those we love the best.
We flatter those we scarcely know,
We please the fleeting guest,
And deal full many a thoughtless blow
To those who love us best.

Ella Wheeler Wilcox

THURSDAY 3

Who's life is it anyway?

Courgette pizza

FROM MAMA RAE

INGREDIENTS
6 medium courgettes
½ cup nutritional yeast
2 minced cloves
1 egg
1 tablespoon oregano
²⁄₃ cup flour
Salt and pepper

THE HOW-TO PART
Grate the courgettes into a bowl. Add the nutritional yeast, minced cloves, egg (beaten), oregano, flour, salt and pepper. When mixed, spread the mixture on a tray and cook for 20 minutes at 180°, flip after 10 minutes. Take out of oven, spread your favourite toppings on top and put back into the oven for 15 minutes.

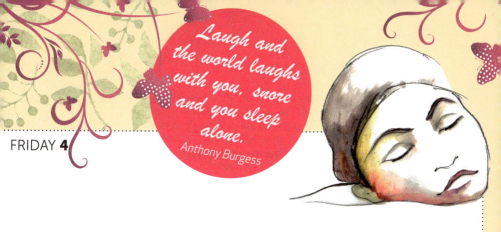

Laugh and the world laughs with you, snore and you sleep alone.
— Anthony Burgess

FRIDAY **4**

Clear out the clutter

SATURDAY **5**

Get up, dress up and show up

SUNDAY **6**

Create good memories

To show your true ability is always, in a sense, to surpass the limits of your ability, to go a little beyond them; to dare, to seek, to invent; it is at such a moment that new talents are revealed, discovered and realised.

Simone de Beauvoir

MAKE THE MOST OF YOUR PRECIOUS LIFE

To celebrate growing older, I once wrote the lessons life taught me.
Life isn't fair, but it's still good.
When in doubt, just that the next small step.
Life is too short to waste time hating anyone.
You don't have to win every argument. Agree to disagree.
It's ok to be angry with God – he can take it.
Your job won't take care of you when you're sick. Stay in touch with friends and family.
Pay off your credit cards every month.
Save for retirement, starting with your first pay cheque.
Make peace with your past so it won't rob you of your future.
It's OK to let your children see you cry.
Don't compare your life to others; you have no idea what their journey is all about.
Envy is a waste of time.
If a relationship has to be a secret, you shouldn't be in it.
Everything can change in the blink of an eye. But don't worry, God never blinks!
When it comes to going after what you want in life, don't take no for an answer.
Burn the candles. Use the nice sheets. Wear the fancy lingerie.
Every day can be a special occasion.
No one is in charge of your happiness but you.
Frame every so-called 'disaster' with "In five years, will this matter?"
Always choose life. Forgive everyone everything.
What other people think of you is none of your business.
Time heals almost everything; give time time.
However good or bad a situation is, it will change.
Don't take yourself too seriously; no one else does.
Believe in miracles.
God loves you because of who God is, not because of anything you did or didn't do.
Growing old beats the alternative – dying young!
No matter how you feel – get up, dress up and show up.
The best is yet to come.
All that truly matters in the end is that you loved.

Regina Brett, 90 years old

MONDAY 7
Bank holiday

Get out of your comfort zone

It is surely wisdom itself to accept wisdom wherever you find it.

People even more than things, have to be restored, renewed, revived, reclaimed and redeemed. Never throw out anyone.

Audrey Hepburn

TUESDAY 8

Help someone else succeed

WEDNESDAY 9

Be happy for no reason

THURSDAY 10

Take positive action

FRIDAY 11

Plan a girls' night in

May

> Alone we can do so little; together we can do so much.
> *Helen Keller*

SATURDAY 12

It's ok to ask for help

SUNDAY 13

Challenge yourself to learn a new skill

> I am a woman in progress. I'm just trying like everybody else. I try to take every conflict, every experience and learn from it. Life is never dull.
> *Oprah Winfrey*

Perfect LOVE casts OUT FEAR
1 John 4:18

> Where love exists, there cannot be conflict of any kind. Peace alone will reign.
> *Amma*

Every person who has ever achieved anything has been knocked down many times. All of them picked themselves up and kept going.

20 TIPS FOR A HEALTHY DAY

1. Rise early and ready to shine.
2. Smile in the mirror as you are brushing your teeth.
3. Break your fast with something substantial.
4. Check your diary and plan your day.
5. Don't neglect important matters in favour of urgent.
6. Drink your greens, avoid the sugars and rotate your foods.
7. Contribute fully to your daily tasks.
8. Drink liquids before or after your meals, not during.
9. Move, move and move some more.
10. Listen to your body – it is wiser than you think.
11. Drink a teaspoon of aloe vera before your main meal to aid digestion.
12. Use herb seasoning (thyme, mint) instead of salt.
13. Decorate your plate and enjoy your food.
14. Eat dinner early; eat smaller meals; eat slowly and chew thoroughly.
15. Eat with good company, even when it's your own.
16. Drink peppermint or fennel tea after your meal.
17. Treat your self to a bath or a good read before bedtime.
18. Early to bed and leave the technology outside the door.
19. Give thanks for the day.
20. Sleep well.

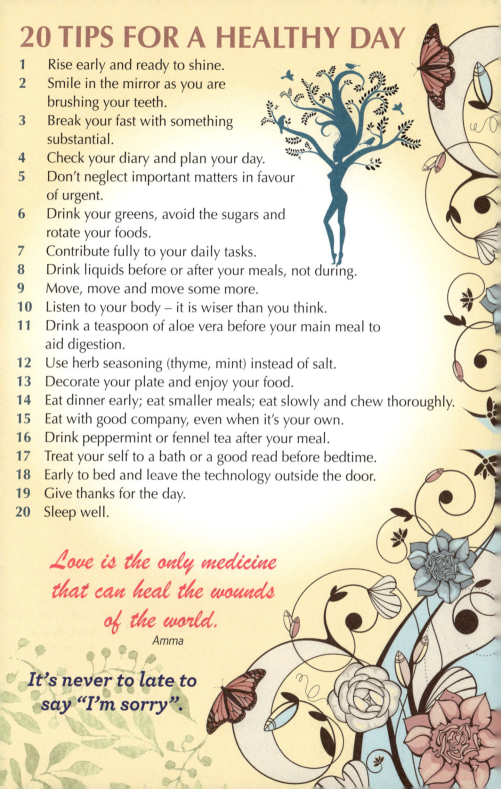

Love is the only medicine that can heal the wounds of the world.
Amma

It's never to late to say "I'm sorry".

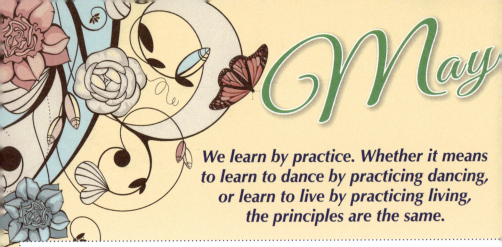

We learn by practice. Whether it means to learn to dance by practicing dancing, or learn to live by practicing living, the principles are the same.

MONDAY **14**

Don't neglect your responsibilities

TUESDAY **15**

Be open to discovering something new

WEDNESDAY **16**

Be grateful for all the good things in your life

THURSDAY **17**

Don't look back in anger or regret

> In order to see growth in your life, you must first see growth in yourself.
> *Emily Gowor*

HAPPY SUMMER TIME

> *We can improve our relationships with others by leaps and bounds if we become encouragers instead of critics.*
> *Joyce Meyer*

FRIDAY 18

This is not a dress rehearsal

SATURDAY 19

Life teaches us to be patient

SUNDAY 20

Thinking is overrated

> If this is coffee, please bring me some tea; but if this is tea, please bring me some coffee.
> *Abraham Lincoln*

May

What others call tough, I call persistent. It's that certain little spirit that compels you stick it out just when you are at your most tired.

Estée Lauder

DOING NOTHING

Do nothing every now and again,
It helps you to relax.
And let your thoughts go wandering
Along some mountain tracks.
Do nothing – it's quite wonderful.
Watch raindrops on the glass,
See the leaves float in the autumn
Sunbeams on the grass,
See the way the clouds keep moving
High above the trees.
Find a little peace and quiet
Moments sure to please.
If your batteries need recharging
And life has lost its smile,
Be still and let the world go by.
Do nothing for a while.

Iris Hesselden

MONDAY 21

Respect your body

TUESDAY 22

Surround yourself with positive people

WEDNESDAY 23

Don't dwell on your mistakes

Honouring and making use of our perceived strengths pays larger dividends than holding ourselves back by our perceived weaknesses.

THURSDAY 24

Acknowledge your accomplishments

FRIDAY 25

Have the courage to be who you really are

SATURDAY 26

Take care of yourself

SUNDAY 27

You are good, you belong and you are not alone

You will never find a better sparring partner than adversity.

Golda Meir

MONDAY 28

Critics are everywhere; beware the one between your ears

TUESDAY 29

Life is full of miracles

WEDNESDAY 30

Eliminate unwanted distractions

THURSDAY 31

For balance, keep it light and flexible

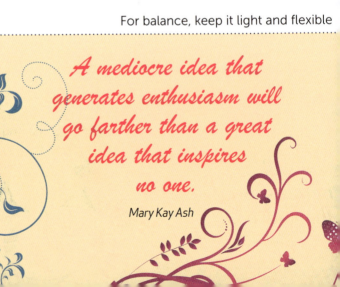

A mediocre idea that generates enthusiasm will go farther than a great idea that inspires no one.

Mary Kay Ash

BUCKET LIST
FOR *June*

I believe that if life gives you lemons, you should make lemonade. And try to find somebody whose life has given them vodka, and have a party.
Ron White

June

> Don't give up trying to do what you really want to do. Where there is love and inspiration, I don't think you can go wrong.
> *Ella Fitzgerald.*

FRIDAY 1

Respect the feelings of others

SATURDAY 2

Look for the win-win option

SUNDAY 3

Respond to a negative situation with a positive intent

> Lord, thou art hard on mothers: We suffer in their coming and their going.
> *Padraig Pearse*

Wear sunscreen

If I could offer you only one tip for the future, sunscreen would be it. The long term benefits of sunscreen have been proved by scientists, whereas the rest of my advice has no basis more reliable than my own meandering experience... I will dispense this advice now.

Enjoy the power and beauty of your youth.

Oh, never mind; you will not understand the power and beauty of your youth until they have faded. But trust me, in 20 years you'll look back at photos of yourself and recall in a way you can't grasp now how much possibility lay before you and how fabulous you really looked.

You're not as fat as you imagine.

Don't worry about the future; or worry, but know that worrying is as effective as trying to solve an algebra equation by chewing bubblegum. The real troubles in your life are apt to be things that never crossed your worried mind. The kind that blindside you at 4pm on some idle Tuesday. Do one thing everyday that scares you.

Sing.

Don't be reckless with other people's hearts, don't put up with people who are reckless with yours.

Floss.

Don't waste your time on jealousy; sometimes you're ahead, sometimes you're behind. The race is long, and in the end, it's only with yourself. Remember the compliments you receive, forget the insults. Keep your old love letters, throw away your old bank statements.

Stretch.

Don't feel guilty if you don't know what you want to do with your Life. The most interesting people I know didn't know at 22 what they wanted to do with their lives, some of the most interesting 40 year olds I know still don't.

Extract from 'Wear Sunscreen', Baz Luhrmann

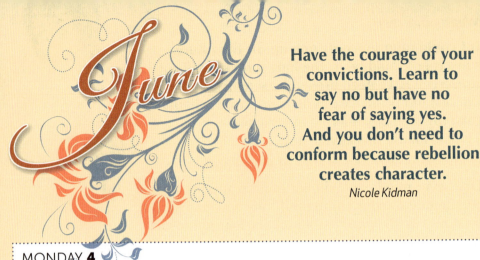

June

> Have the courage of your convictions. Learn to say no but have no fear of saying yes. And you don't need to conform because rebellion creates character.
> *Nicole Kidman*

MONDAY 4
Bank holiday

You can't achieve greatness by yourself

TUESDAY 5

Organise to reduce stress

WEDNESDAY 6

Avoid negative people

THURSDAY 7

Clear decisions make life easier

> Old friends pass away, new friends appear.
> It is just like the days. An old day passes, a new day arrives.
> The important thing is to make it meaningful:
> a meaningful friend – or a meaningful day.
> *Dalai Lama*

FRIDAY 8

Choose to act not simply react

SATURDAY 9

Your body hears everything your mind says

SUNDAY 10

Stay true to your purpose

SIX ESSENTIAL BEAUTY TIPS FOR BUSY WOMEN

1. Get a fantastic haircut.
2. Use a multi-purpose complexion and SPF product tinted moisturiser or BB cream.
3. Take advantage of dry shampoo.
4. Don't forget the mascara (or tint your eyelashes).
5. Use lip gloss.
6. Put on cream blush.

We gain strength, and courage, and confidence by each experience in which we really stop to look fear in the face. we must do that which we think we cannot do.
Eleanor Roosevelt

MONDAY 11

Invest in yourself

TUESDAY 12

Give yourself permission to go for what you really want

WEDNESDAY 13

Say yes first, then figure out how

THURSDAY 14

Be a trailblazer

FRIDAY 15

Don't sell out on yourself

June

Citrus banana icecream
FROM MAMA RAE

INGREDIENTS
3 bananas
2 oranges, juiced
2 lemons, juiced
2 cups almond milk/or your milk of your choice
½ cup of sugar, or to taste

THE HOW-TO PART
Put the bananas into a bowl and mash them.
Add the sugar and stir to dissolve.
Add the orange and lemon juice and finally the milk.
Stir until it is mixed through.
Pour into a dish and place in the freezer.
Each hour or so give the ice-cream a stir.
You can eat it when it has lots of ice crystals. Enjoy!

PRAYER OF A SPORTS MOM

Lord, Help me remember I'm having fun –
the chaos, the rushing, the meals on the run.
Don't let us forget the equipment we need,
and not get delayed so I don't have to speed.
May I cheer even if my child is benched, or
it's raining or snowing and I'm cold and drenched.
and may I not, right in mid-game, stop to think
"oh no, I forgot, it's my day for drinks!"
For I know it's important to show my support.
to be there for my kids, as their youth is so short.
I thank you for having this time with them Lord ...
for being a Sports Mom is its own reward.

It is not the horse that draws the cart, but the oats.

Russian Proverb

Stay connected to what makes you feel most alive

It isn't where you come from, it's where you're going that counts.
Ella Fitzgerald

June

SATURDAY 16

Recognise your bad habits

SUNDAY 17
Father's Day

Don't worry about it being perfect, just get it started

> People are like stained glass windows. They sparkle and shine when the sun is out, but when the darkness sets in, their true beauty is revealed only if there is a light from within.
>
> *Elisabeth Kubler Ross*

> **Sometimes you can't see yourself clearly until you see yourself through the eyes of others.**
> *Ellen de Generes*

MONDAY 18

Break big goals into smaller tasks

TUESDAY 19

There is an upside to every situation

WEDNESDAY 20

Develop self-reliance

THURSDAY 21

Be willing to change a losing formula

> **It is wonderful how much time good people spend fighting the devil. If they would only expend the same amount of energy loving their fellow men, the devil would die in his own tracks of ennui.**
> *Helen Keller*

> The purpose of life is to live it, to taste experience to the utmost, to reach out eagerly and without fear for newer and richer experience.
> — *Eleanor Roosevelt*

June

FRIDAY 22

Check **www.getupandgoevents.com** for details of upcoming Get Up and Go event

SATURDAY 23

Do your best with what you have

SUNDAY 24

Create balance in your mind and bring it to your life

Cocktail "Kamikaze"

3 cl Vodka
3 cl Triple Sec
3 cl Lime Juice

> Turns out you have a really fun time if you go to work every day and focus on being silly and funny and happy!
> — *Hannah Murray*

If you truly put your heart into what you believe in, even if it makes you vulnerable, amazing things can and will happen.
Emma Watson

MONDAY 25

Playing small does not serve the world

TUESDAY 26

Have the courage to fight for what you believe in

WEDNESDAY 27

Nothing positive comes from worry

THURSDAY 28

Keep your environment positive

Someone who points out your flaws to you is not necessarily your enemy. Someone who speaks of your virtues is not necessarily your friend.

Delicious smoothie

1 medium ripe banana, sliced.
1 cup fresh pineapple, diced.
½ cup fresh strawberries.
¾ cup milk.
1 Tbsp honey or agave nectar.
6 ice cubes or 1 cup crushed ice.
Whipped cream, chocolate syrup, and a maraschino cherry for garnish.

Blend the pineapple and strawberry in a blender until mashed. Add the other ingredients and blend on high until smooth. Pour into two frozen parfait, coupe, or glass of your choice. Top with a dollop of whipped cream, a drizzle of chocolate syrup, and a maraschino cherry.

For fast-acting relief, try slowing down.

Life shrinks or expands in proportion to ones courage.
— Anais Nin

FRIDAY 29

Choose freely and accept the consequences

SATURDAY 30

Life is a balancing act

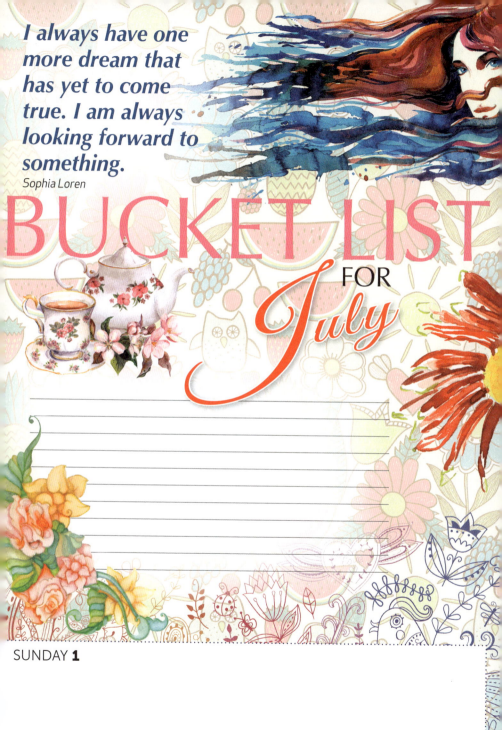

I always have one more dream that has yet to come true. I am always looking forward to something.
Sophia Loren

BUCKET LIST
FOR
July

SUNDAY 1

What ever game you're playing, be a good sport!

I always wanted to be somebody, but now I realise I should have been more specific.

Lily Tomlin

MONDAY 2

There is no such thing as 'having it all'

TUESDAY 3

Schedule regular downtime

WEDNESDAY 4

Keep everything in perspective

THURSDAY 5

We become like the people we regularly associate with

FRIDAY 6

Do more of what you love

July

SIX UNDENIABLE FACTS OF LIFE

1. Don't educate your children to be rich. Educate them to be happy. So when they grow up they will know the value of things not the price.
2. Best awarded words: "Eat your food as your medicines. Otherwise you have to eat medicines as your food."
3. The one who loves you will never leave you – because even if there are 100 reasons to give up, he or she will find one reason to hold on.
4. There is a big difference between a human being and being human. Only a few really understand it.
5. You are loved when you are born. You will be loved when you die. In between, you have to manage!
6. If you just want to walk fast, walk alone, but if you want to walk far, walk together!

SATURDAY 7

We are empowered by empowering others

SUNDAY 8

Don't worry too much about what other people think

July

Stifling an urge to dance is bad for your health – it rusts your spirit and your hips.

Adabella Radici

Choc chip slice

FROM MAMA RAE

INGREDIENTS
1 can chickpeas
½ cup almond butter
⅓ cup maple syrup
1 teaspoon vanilla
¼ teaspoon baking powder
¼ teaspoon baking soda
¼ teaspoon salt
½ cup choc chips

THE HOW-TO PART
Drain and rinse the chickpeas, process in food processor with almond butter, maple syrup, vanilla, baking powder, baking soda and salt. Add ¼ cup choc chips and stir in. Pour into slice tin and smooth. Sprinkle ¼ cup choc chips on the top and press down. Bake for 30-35 minutes at 175 degrees

MAMA RAE'S INSIDE SECRETS
You can use any of the nut butters, it doesn't affect the taste. Substitute your favourite sweetener for the maple syrup.

MONDAY 9

Have people in your life who make you laugh

TUESDAY 10

Stand up for what is right

WEDNESDAY 11

Do something that makes a positive difference

> Accept the children the way we accept trees – with gratitude, because they are a blessing – but do not have expectations or desires. You don't expect trees to change, you love them as they are.
>
> *Isabel Allende*

THURSDAY 12

Forgive yourself

FRIDAY 13

Celebrate the 'little wins'

SATURDAY 14

Collaborate where possible

SUNDAY 15

Love your job

July

If you want children to keep their feet on the ground, put some responsibility on their shoulders.

MONDAY 16

Live your biggest life

TUESDAY 17

Trust your intuition

WEDNESDAY 18

Value your own opinions

THURSDAY 19

Give more than is expected

I have no need to be average or normal. I surrender the need to fit in to the expectations of others at the expense of my own evolution. I joyfully celebrate my loss of normalcy, and claim my authenticity, sanity and health.

Epstein

FRIDAY 20

Let go of the need to control

SATURDAY 21

Don't let your fears hold you back

SUNDAY 22

Check www.getupandgoevents.com for details of upcoming Get Up and Go event

It's difficult to ever go back to the same places or people. You turn away, even for a moment, and when you turn back around, everything's changed.

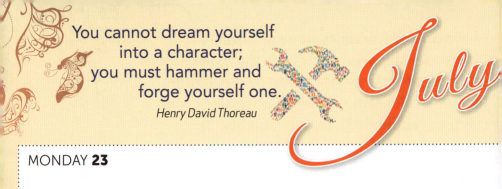

> You cannot dream yourself into a character; you must hammer and forge yourself one.
> — *Henry David Thoreau*

July

MONDAY 23

Let go of the baggage that is weighing you down

As we grow older, and hence wiser, we slowly realise that a $300 or a $30 watch both tell the same time. Whether we carry a $300 or a $30 wallet/handbag, the amount of money inside is the same. Whether we drink a bottle of $300 or $10 wine – the hangover is the same. Whether the house we live in is 300 or 3,000 sq ft, loneliness is the same. You will realise that your true inner happiness does not come from the material things of this world. Therefore, when you have mates, buddies and old friends, brothers and sisters, who you chat with, laugh with, talk with, have sung songs with, and talk about north-south-east-west or heaven and earth ... that is true happiness!

TUESDAY 24

It takes courage to choose to change

Be fearless. Have the courage to take risks. Go where there are no guarantees. Get out of your comfort zone. Get comfortable with being uncomfortable.

WEDNESDAY 25

Don't make assumptions

THURSDAY 26

Forgive a friend for a perceived hurt

FRIDAY 27

Love yourself just the way you are

SATURDAY 28

Sometimes criticism is constructive

SUNDAY 29

Peace begins in your own heart

WHEN YOU THOUGHT I WASN'T LOOKING
(POEM FOR MOTHERS)

July

A message every adult should read because children are watching you and doing as you do, not as you say.

When you thought I wasn't looking, I saw you hang my first painting on the refrigerator and I immediately wanted to paint another one.
When you thought I wasn't looking, I saw you feed a stray cat and I learned that it was good to be kind to animals.
When you thought I wasn't looking, I saw you make my favorite cake for me and I learned that the little things can be the special things in life.
When you thought I wasn't looking, I heard you say a prayer and I knew that there is a God I could always talk to, and I learned to trust in him.
When you thought I wasn't looking, I saw you make a meal and take it to a friend who was sick and I learned that we all have to help take care of each other.
When you thought I wasn't looking, I saw you give of your time and money to help people who had nothing and I learned that those who have something should give to those who don't.
When you thought I wasn't looking, I saw you take care of our house and everyone in it and I learned we have to take care of what we are given.
When you thought I wasn't looking, I saw how you handled your responsibilities, even when you didn't feel good and I learned that I would have to be responsible when I grow up.
When you thought I wasn't looking, I saw tears come from your eyes and I learned that sometimes things hurt, but it's all right to cry.
When you thought I wasn't looking, I saw that you cared and I wanted to be everything that I could be.
When you thought I wasn't looking, I learned most of life's lessons that I need to know to be a good and productive person when I grow up.
When you thought I wasn't looking I looked at you and wanted to say, 'Thanks for all the things I saw when you thought I wasn't looking.

10 things to remember

1. The past cannot be changed but your view of the past can.
2. Opinions don't define reality, they simply express someone's view of their reality.
3. Everyones journey is different, concentrate on your own and remember it's a journey!
4. Judgements are a confession of your own character
5. Overthinking will lead to anxiety.
6. Happiness is found within when you serve without expecting return.
7. Positive thoughts lead to positive actions and positive results.
8. Smiles are contagious and kindness is free.
9. You only fail when you say you fail.
10. What goes around comes around.

MONDAY 30

Give up the struggle and dance with life

TUESDAY 31

Take control of your financial situation

With every act of self care your authentic self gets stronger, and the critical, fearful mind gets weaker. Every act of self care is a powerful declaration: I am on my side; each day I am more and more on my side.

Susan Weiss Berry

BUCKET LIST FOR *August*

You have set yourselves a difficult task, but you will succeed if you persevere, and you will find a joy in overcoming obstacles. Remember, no effort that we make to attain something beautiful is ever lost. What I am looking for is not out there, it is in me.

Remember, you have been criticising yourself for years and it hasn't worked. Try approving of yourself and see what happens.

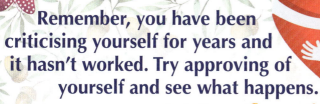

Louise Hay

We should all start to live before we get too old. Fear is stupid. So are regrets.

Marilyn Monroe.

The secret to happiness is letting every situation be what it is, instead of what you think it should be.

Love is friendship that has caught fire. It is quiet understanding, mutual confidence, sharing and forgiving. It is loyalty through good and bad times. It settles for less than perfection and makes allowances for human weaknesses.

Ann Landers

At the end of the day, we can endure much more than we think we can.

Frida Kahlo

WEDNESDAY **1**

Find the good in the imperfect

August

Maybe you'll marry, maybe you won't, maybe you'll have children, maybe you won't, maybe you'll divorce at 40, maybe you'll dance the funky chicken on your 75th wedding anniversary. Whatever you do, don't congratulate yourself too much or berate yourself either. Your choices are half-chance, so are everybody else's.

Enjoy your body – use it every way you can. Don't be afraid of it, or what other people think of it. It's the greatest instrument you'll ever own. Dance, even if you have nowhere to do it but in your own living room. Do not read beauty magazines, they will only make you feel ugly.

Get to know your parents, you never know when they'll be gone for good. Be nice to your siblings –they are the best link to your past and the people most likely to stick with you in the future. Understand that friends come and go, but for the precious few you should hold on. Travel.

Accept certain inalienable truths: prices will rise, politicians will philander, you too will get old, and when you do you'll fantasize that when you were young prices were reasonable, politicians were noble and children respected their elders.

Respect your elders. Don't expect anyone else to support you. Maybe you have a trust fund or maybe you have a wealthy spouse, but you never know when either one might run out. Don't mess too much with your hair, or by the time you're 40, it will look 85.

Extract from 'Wear Sunscreen',
Baz Luhrmann

The best work is done with the heart breaking, or overflowing.
Mignon McLoughlin

Time spent with cats is never wasted.
Sigmund Freud

THURSDAY **2**

Stop feeling guilty – it's unproductive!

FRIDAY **3**

Value your unique contribution

SATURDAY **4**

Love your life

SUNDAY **5**

Stop waiting for the world to make you happy – it's a DIY job

August

> *We'd achieve more if we chased our dreams instead of our competition.*
> Simon Sinek

MONDAY 6
Bank holiday

Enjoy the fruits of a healthy lifestyle

TUESDAY 7

Have the strength to try again

WEDNESDAY 8

Learn to experience and appreciate the present moment

THURSDAY 9

Welcome the unexpected

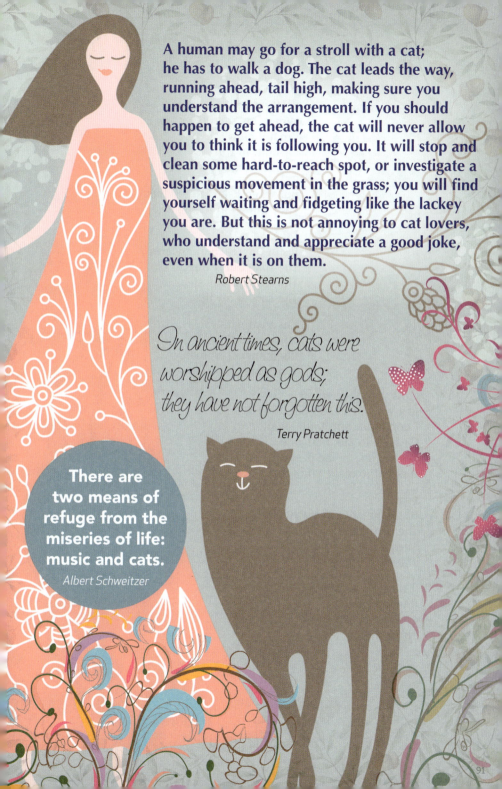

A human may go for a stroll with a cat; he has to walk a dog. The cat leads the way, running ahead, tail high, making sure you understand the arrangement. If you should happen to get ahead, the cat will never allow you to think it is following you. It will stop and clean some hard-to-reach spot, or investigate a suspicious movement in the grass; you will find yourself waiting and fidgeting like the lackey you are. But this is not annoying to cat lovers, who understand and appreciate a good joke, even when it is on them.
Robert Stearns

In ancient times, cats were worshipped as gods; they have not forgotten this.
Terry Pratchett

There are two means of refuge from the miseries of life: music and cats.
Albert Schweitzer

August

Pretty women wonder
Where my secret lies
I'm not cute
Or built to suit
A fashion model's size.

But when I start to tell them,
They think I'm telling lies.

I say...
It's in the reach of my arms,
The span of my hips,
The stride of my step,
The curl of my lips.

I'm a woman,
Phenomenally.
Phenomenal woman,
That's me.

Now you understand
Just why my head's not bowed,
I don't shout or jump about
Or have to talk real loud.
When you see me passing,
It ought to make you proud

I say...
It's in the click of my heels,
The bend of my hair,
The palm of my hand,
The need of my care.

'Cause I'm a woman,
Phenomenally.
Phenomenal woman,
That's me.

Don't waste your time on work that you don't enjoy. You cannot succeed in something that you don't like. Patience, passion, and dedication come easily only when you love what you do.

> When you reach for the stars, you are reaching for the farthest thing out there. When you reach deep into yourself, it is the same thing, but in the opposite direction. If you reach in both directions, you will have spanned the universe.
> *Vera Nazarian*

FRIDAY **10**

Pay attention to what matters most

SATURDAY **11**

Everyone deserves to be heard

> *Love is a fire. But whether it is going to warm your hearth or burn down your house, you can never tell.*
> Joan Crawford

SUNDAY **12**

This too will pass

August

I long to accomplish a great and noble task, but it is my chief duty to accomplish small tasks as if they were great and noble. The world is moved along, not only by the mighty shoves of its heroes, but also the aggregate of the tiny pushes of each honest worker.

MONDAY **13**

Nurture the relationships you have

TUESDAY **14**

Multitasking takes its toll

WEDNESDAY **15**

Give the person you are with your full attention

THURSDAY **16**

Be willing to laugh at yourself, and at life

The quickest way for a parent to get a child's attention is to sit down and look comfortable.

FRIDAY 17

Be a good listener

SATURDAY 18

Use your time wisely – this moment will not come again

Meditation is both the symbol and expression of our intention to grow. Sitting still, alone with our thoughts and feelings, we can honor missed opportunities, passing desires, remembered disappointments, as well as our inner strength, personal wisdom, and ability to forgive and love.

Sebastian Pole

SUNDAY 19

You do not have to prove yourself to anyone

Appreciate the people around you. Your friends and relatives will always be an infinite source of strength and love. That is why you shouldn't take them for granted.

MONDAY 20

Take time out for yourself every day

TUESDAY 21

Allow for wonder in your life

WEDNESDAY 22

Only complain to someone who can do something about it

THURSDAY 23

Check **www.getupandgoevents.com** for details of upcoming Get Up and Go event

I think all women feel guilty. I think what's interesting is, I dont know many men who feel guilty.

Sheryl Sandberg

August

Choc banana pudding
FROM MAMA RAE

INGREDIENTS
6 cups of bread
3 ripe bananas
2-2¼ cups milk
3 tablespoons flour
⅓ cup maple syrup
1 teaspoon vanilla
½ teaspoon cinnamon
1/1¼ teaspoon nutmeg
1 cup choc chips

THE HOW-TO PART
Turn oven on to 180 degrees. Tear the bread into small pieces into a bowl. Whisk the milk, vanilla and flour, cinnamon and nutmeg. Add the maple syrup and stir. Pour over bread. Stir in mashed bananas and choc chips. Pour into a 9 x 5inch dish and bake for 30 minutes.

MAMA RAE'S INSIDE SECRETS
Omit the maple syrup and add six chopped dates.
Use two bananas and ½ cup dried apricots or peaches.
It is also yummy with ½ cup slivered almonds.

FRIDAY 24

Think big, aim high, act bold

SATURDAY 25

Be open to opportunity

SUNDAY 26

Look around and take notice – all is not as it seems

MONDAY 27

Turn your can'ts into cans and your won'ts into wills

TUESDAY 28

Stay away from the Cudda Wudda Shudda sisters

WEDNESDAY 29

Great questions lead the way to great answers

THURSDAY 30

Be gentle with yourself

> *I have always adored beautiful young men. Just because I grow older, my taste doesn't change. So, if I can still have them, why not?*
> Bridget Bardot

FRIDAY 31

Give the gift of your happiness to your friends and family

It's nonsense to be afraid of others' opinions. Some people may think you crazy, while others may think you're a legend. You're the only one who's opinion of you matters.

BUCKET LIST FOR *September*

CHILDREN LEARN WHAT THEY LIVE

If children live with criticism, they learn to condemn.
If children live with hostility, they learn to fight.
If children live with ridicule, they learn to be shy.
If children live with shame, they learn to feel guilty.
If children live with patience, they learn to be tolerant.
If children live with encouragement, they learn confidence.
If children live with praise, they learn to appreciate.
If children live with fairness, they learn justice.
If children live with security, they learn to have faith.
If children live with approval, they learn to like themselves.
If children live with acceptance and friendship,
they learn that there is love in the world.

Nachos with beans and chickpeas
FROM MAMA RAE

INGREDIENTS
1 can black beans
1 can chickpeas
1 onion
1 clove garlic
1 teaspoon ground ginger
1 teaspoon turmeric
1 teaspoon cumin
½ teaspoon cinnamon
¼ teaspoon ground cloves
Chilli to taste
425gm diced tomatoes
Corn chips

THE HOW-TO PART
Smash the black beans and chickpeas into a bowl. Chop the onion and finely chop the garlic. Saute in 2 – 3 tablespoons water for three minutes. Add the ginger, turmeric, cumin, cinnamon, ground cloves and chilli. Add the diced tomatoes. Stir through and simmer for 20 minutes. Serve with corn chips and any of the following: smashed avocado, pesto, sweet potato hummus, salsa, nut cheese, or yoghurt.

MAMA RAE'S INSIDE SECRETS
You can use other beans: cannellini, red kidney, butter beans, pinto and navy beans. If you don't have diced tomatoes then add half a bottle of passata and a chopped tomato. Use two teaspoons of curry instead of the spices.

September

Even today the most jaded city dweller can be unexpectedly moved upon encountering a clear night sky studded with thousands of twinkling stars.

SATURDAY 1

Have a mind open to new ideas

SUNDAY 2

Don't wait – the time will never be just right

> I believe art is utterly important. It is one of the things that could save us. We don't have to rely totally on experience if we can do things in our imagination.... It's the only way in which you can live more lives than your own. You can escape your own time, your own sensibility, your own narrowness of vision.
>
> *Mary Oliver*

September

MONDAY 3

There are unlimited possibilities 'locked' inside you

TUESDAY 4

Discover your Why and you can figure the How

WEDNESDAY 5

Be ok with chaos

THURSDAY 6

We all have the capacity for recuperation and repair

> **Every positive value has its price in negative terms... the genius of Einstein leads to Hiroshima.**
> *Pablo Picasso*

20 foods to boost your immune system

1. Broccoli
2. Brown rice
3. Cabbage
4. Nuts
5. Ginger
6. Garlic
7. Lemon
8. Chicken soup
9. Honey
10. Mushrooms
11. Oats
12. Spinach
13. Oysters
14. Salmon
15. Tomatoes
16. Sweet potatoes
17. Watermelon
18. Wheatgerm
19. Water
20. Yoghurt

FRIDAY 7

All will be well

SATURDAY 8

Time is a great healer; give time time

SUNDAY 9

Go with the flow or expect adversity

> *You can't build a reputation on what you are going to do.*
> Henry Ford

MONDAY 10

Forgiveness is the only access to peace

TUESDAY 11

Beware of starting what you might later regret

WEDNESDAY 12

Growth and development is never a done deal

THURSDAY 13

Practice compassion

FRIDAY 14

Make a list of your best qualities and display it

September

Business is not something to be lightly tried on. It's not a distraction, not an affair, not a momentary fling. Business marries you. You sleep with it, eat with it, think about it much of your time. It is in a very real sense, an act of love. If it isn't an act of love, it's merely work, not business.
Estee Lauder

hope

We can do anything we want as long as we stick to it long enough.

It is your turn now, you waited, you were patient. The time has come for us to polish you. We will transform your inner pearl into a house of fire. You're a gold mine, did you know that, hidden in the dirt of the earth? It is your turn now to be placed in fire.
Rumi

Never give up!

SATURDAY 15

Widen your circle of friends

SUNDAY 16

Within a crisis are the seeds of a new opportunity

MONDAY **17**

Attract what you want into your life

TUESDAY **18**

Make your life your masterpiece

> We are supposed to enjoy the good stuff now, while we can, with the people we love. Life has a funny way of teaching us that lesson over and over again.
> *Sheena Easton*

> *You are braver than you believe, stronger than you seem, and smarter than you think.*
> Winnie the Pooh

WEDNESDAY **19**

Take the initiative

September

> Gratitude unlocks the fullness of life. It turns what we have into enough, and more. It turns denial into acceptance, chaos to order, confusion to clarity. It can turn a meal into a feast, a house into a home, a stranger into a friend.
>
> *Melody Beattie*

THURSDAY 20

You cannot be walked on if you are not lying down

FRIDAY 21

Don't believe everything you hear

SATURDAY 22

You are responsible for the quality of your own experience

SUNDAY 23

'I can' and 'I will' is a way of life

September

MONDAY 24

Don't engage in 'pity-parties'

TUESDAY 25

Healthy relationships require constant maintenance

WEDNESDAY 26

Accept things as they are

> Love and respect a woman. Look to her not only for comfort, but for strength and inspiration and the doubling of your intellectual and moral powers. Blot out from your mind any idea of superiority; you have none.
>
> *Giuseppe Mazzini*

There is a vitality, a life force, an energy, a quickening that is translated through you into action, and because there is only one of you, in all of time, this expression is unique. If you block it, it will never exist and be lost to the world.

Every experience has a lesson.
Every situation has a silver lining.

THURSDAY 27

Look people in the eye when you speak to them

FRIDAY 28

Follow your heart

SATURDAY 29

Write a letter to someone who has helped you

SUNDAY 30

Fix the problem not the blame

Good friends walk in when the old ones walk out.

BUCKET LIST
FOR
October

Wear your art like your heart on your sleeve and keep it alive by making people feel a little better, a little lighter, a little more love. Create art in order for yourself to become yourself and let your very existence be your song, your poem, your story. Let the way people say your name sound like the sweetest melody.

Don't talk about yourself; it will be done when you leave.

MONDAY 1

Do not complain about what you permit

It is not only for what we do that we are held responsible, but also for what we do not do.
— Moliere

TUESDAY 2

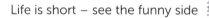

Life is short – see the funny side

WEDNESDAY 3

Inside you is the key to everything you can imagine

THURSDAY 4

Set an example buy being loving, peaceful and kind

October

Pumpkin and chickpea curry
FROM MAMA RAE

INGREDIENTS
1 teaspoon cumin seeds
1 cinnamon stick
1 large onion
4 cloves garlic
1 red chilli
1½ teaspoons garam masala
½ teaspoon turmeric
270ml coconut milk
1.2kg pumpkin
2 cans chickpeas
150gm spinach
1 tablespoon lemon juice

THE HOW-TO PART
Chop onion and chilli (no seeds). Cut pumpkin into 2.5cm cubes. Saute onion in 2 – 3 tablespoons water for 5 minutes add the spices stirring for 2 minutes. Add coconut milk and pumpkin stirring to coat the pumpkin. Cook until pumpkin is just tender adding chickpeas in the last 5 minutes. Add lemon juice and mix. Lastly add the spinach cover the pot and let the spinach wilt.

MAMA RAE'S INSIDE SECRETS
You can substitute sweet potato for pumpkin.
For a mild curry leave out the chilli.

FRIDAY 5

Be punctual

SATURDAY 6

Read the instructions

SUNDAY 7

Make a list of what needs to be done

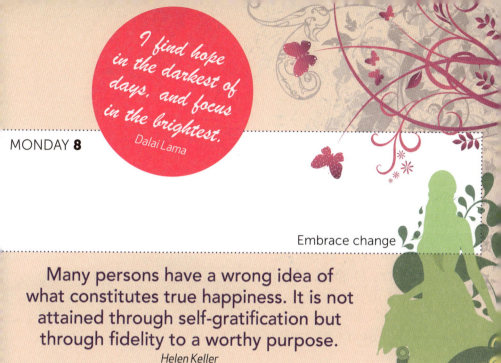

MONDAY 8

I find hope in the darkest of days, and focus in the brightest.
— Dalai Lama

Embrace change

> Many persons have a wrong idea of what constitutes true happiness. It is not attained through self-gratification but through fidelity to a worthy purpose.
> — Helen Keller

TUESDAY 9

Schedule a weekly 30 minute tech detox

WEDNESDAY 10

Never seek revenge

THURSDAY 11

Hot tempers cool friendships

October

So go create.
Take photographs in the wood,
run alone in the rain and sing your
heart out high up on a mountain
where no one will ever hear
and your very existence will
be the most hypnotising scar.
Make your life be your art
and you will never be forgotten.

Charlotte Eriksson

FRIDAY 12

See problems as challenges

SATURDAY 13

Cheer yourself up by cheering someone else up

SUNDAY 14

Take a good look in the mirror – and love what you see

MONDAY 15

Never give up

> *The face is the mirror of the mind, and eyes without speaking confess the secrets of the heart.*
> St Jerome

TUESDAY 16

Everyone's opinion is valid

WEDNESDAY 17

Don't waste your time on regrets

THURSDAY 18

Don't make promises you are not going to keep

FRIDAY 19

Think of ways to improve your future

October

I have never been hurt by what I have not said.
— Calvin Coolidge

I stood willingly and gladly in the characters of everything – other people, trees, clouds. And this is what I learned, that the world's otherness is antidote to confusion – that standing within this otherness – the beauty and the mystery of the world, out in the fields or deep inside books – can re-dignify the worst-stung heart.
— Mary Oliver

SATURDAY 20

Trust life to be wonderful

SUNDAY 21

Families are great training grounds

If you cannot get rid of the family skeleton, you may as well teach it to dance.
— George Bernard Shaw

Your success and happiness lives in you.

MONDAY 22

Don't procrastinate; do it now

TUESDAY 23

Seek to understand first, then to be understood

WEDNESDAY 24

Honesty is always the best policy

THURSDAY 25

Be happy in the moment of now

FRIDAY 26

You are doing a great job

October

YOU HAVE A GIFT

It's the gift of a mind that is capable of truly remarkable endeavors. Miraculous even.

You see, your IQ doesn't define you. Your salary doesn't define you. Likewise, your level of fitness, your current career position, and your number of friends don't define who you are either.

Rather, greatness does exist within you. Incredible ability is there, just waiting to be tapped. You're on the cusp of realising fantastic achievements. And it's all within your mind … and it's all within your reach!

So the question has never been "Do you have the skills, the talent, and the ability to be great?"

The question is: "How will you begin to reveal your greatness, your gift, right now?"

SATURDAY 27

Try and fail but don't fail to try

SUNDAY 28

Put faith in your attitude, not in your circumstances

MONDAY 29
Bank holiday

Compose a mission statement for your life

TUESDAY 30

Live your life with passion and purpose

WEDNESDAY 31

Be patient with children

It wasn't youth that made me so energetic; it was enthusiasm. That's why I know a woman of any age has it within her to begin a business or life work of any sort. It's a fresh outlook thats makes youth so attractive anyway, that quality of 'anything's possible'.
Estee Lauder

Darkness soothes. It softens the sharp edges of the world, toned down the too-harsh colors. With the coming of twilight, the sky seems to recede; the universe to expand. The night seems bigger than the day, and in its realm, like the stars that come out to shine, life seems to have infinitely more possibilities.

> *Others have seen what is and asked why. I have seen what could be and asked why not.*
> — Pablo Picasso

BUCKET LIST FOR November

THURSDAY 1

Light a candle in memory of someone you loved and lost

THE GENTLE LIFESTYLE

Gentleness is thinking gentle thoughts about yourself, others and life.
Gentleness is feeling the energy of gentle love filling one's whole being and flowing out to the world.
Gentleness is listening attentively to each person with gentle love.
Gentleness is speaking gently so that what you say will encourage and do good for others.
Gentleness is doing the loving thing as we work for a better, more just and caring world.
Gentleness is an awareness of our fragility and taking care of our health and wellbeing in mind and body.
Gentleness is a willingness to see an opportunity in every difficulty.
Gentleness is the way of gratitude for all that we have.
Gentleness is the humble acceptance of ourselves with all our weaknesses.
Gentleness is the strength that quietly acknowledges our unique place in the world.

FRIDAY 2

Don't let this crazy world spin you out of control

SATURDAY 3

Self acceptance is the key to happiness

SUNDAY 4

There is nothing to be gained by putting yourself down

November

THE HEALTH-FOOD DINER

No sprouted wheat and soya shoots
And Brussels in a cake,
Carrot straw and spinach raw,
(Today, I need a steak).
Not thick brown rice and rice pilau
Or mushrooms creamed on toast,
Turnips mashed and parsnips hashed,
(I'm dreaming of a roast).
Health-food folks around the world
Are thinned by anxious zeal,
They look for help in seafood kelp
(I count on breaded veal).
No smoking signs,
Raw mustard greens,
Zucchini by the ton,
Uncooked kale and bodies frail
Are sure to make me run to
Loins of pork and chicken thighs
And standing rib, so prime,
Pork chops brown and fresh ground round
(I crave them all the time).
Irish stews and boiled corned beef
And hot dogs by the scores,
Or any place that saves a space
For smoking carnivores.

Maya Angelou

*Beauty to me is about
being comfortable in your own ski
That or a kick ass red lipstick.*

Gwyneth Paltrow

Chicken wings with bean shoots

FROM MAMA RAE

INGREDIENTS
6 spring onions
2 cloves garlic
2 tablespoons soy sauce
2 tablespoons sherry
1 teaspoon ginger
1 tablespoon honey
750gm chicken wings
1 teaspoon chicken stock powder
2 teaspoons flour
¾ cup water
345gm bean shoots

THE HOW-TO PART
Slice the spring onions and chop the garlic.
Stir in the soy sauce, sherry, ginger and honey. Add the chicken wings to marinade, chill for at least an hour, turning wings. Mix the stock powder, flour and water to a paste and stir into marinade. Bake at 175º for 35–40 minutes. Fry the bean shoots in a little oil until brown. Add to wings five minutes before cooked.

MAMA RAE'S INSIDE SECRETS
You can do the marinade in the morning and turn the wings three or four times during the day. You can use drumsticks instead of wings. Water chestnuts works well also. Slice them thinly.

MONDAY 5

Life is all about chances, choices and changes

TUESDAY 6

Courage and confidence come from within

WEDNESDAY 7

Put your dreams to work for you

THURSDAY 8

Let your light shine

November

Anyone who says he can see through women is missing a lot.

Groucho Marx

FRIDAY 9

Be a supportive friend

SATURDAY 10

Plan a romantic dinner by candlelight

SUNDAY 11

We each have the best of us at the heart of us

The worst sin toward our fellow creatures is not to hate them, but to be indifferent to them: that's the essence of inhumanity.

George Bernard Shaw

> *It takes considerable knowledge just to realise the extent of your own ignorance.*
> *Thomas Sowell*

MONDAY 12

Be content within yourself

TUESDAY 13

If it doesn't challenge you it wont change you

WEDNESDAY 14

The world is truly an amazing place

THURSDAY 15

The more you look the more you see

FRIDAY 16

Be clear on your ground rules

November

WHEN I'M A LITTLE OLD LADY
(POEM FOR MOTHERS)

I'll live with my children and bring them great joy
To repay all I have had from each girl and boy.
I shall draw on the walls and scuff up the floor,
Run in and out without closing the door.
I'll hide frogs in the pantry, socks under my bed,
Whenever they scold me, I'll just hang my head.
I'll run and I'll romp, always fritter away
The time to be spent doing chores every day.
I'll pester my children when they're on the phone,
As long as they're busy, I won't leave them alone.
I'll hide candy in closets, rocks in a drawer
And never pick up my clothes from the floor.
I'll dash off to the movies and not wash a dish,
I'll plead for allowance whenever I wish.
I'll stuff up the plumbing and deluge the floor,
As soon as they've mopped it, I'll flood it some more.
When they correct me, I'll lie down and cry,
Kicking and screaming, not a tear in my eye.
I'll take all their pencils and flashlights, and then
When they buy new ones, I'll take them again.
I'll spill glasses of milk to complete every meal,
Eat my banana and just drop the peel.
Put toys on the table, spill jam on the floor,
I'll break lots of dishes as though I were four.
What fun I shall have! What joy it will be!
To live with my children – like they lived with me!

Author unknown

SIX THINGS TO PRACTICE DAILY

1. SAY THANK YOU. Studies have shown that people who express gratitude are least likely to experience depression and have an easier time managing the ups and downs of life. Take a minute every day to be grateful for all that is positive in your life.

2. TAKE A WALK. Not only is it good for you physically, walking can also elevate your mood and get you back to center fast! Even a stroll for 15 minutes a day can do wonders.

3. INDULGE IN A BOOK. When is the last time you fell in love with a character in a book? Not only can reading take our minds off of immediate stress and pressure it can help maintain healthy cognitive functions; a good book is a great thing to go to when under stress!

4. SAVOUR A YUMMY TREAT. Both dark chocolate and red wine contain Reservatrol which is believed to stave off cancer and heart disease, contribute to longevity and boost your metabolism. Go ahead, have a (one!) glass of red wine or nibble on a piece of dark chocolate – it's actually good for you! In convivial company it's even better!

5. SAY NO. You may be feeling overextended because you say yes to things you think you should do, but don't actually want to do. Being comfortable in saying no is key to preserving a healthy mental state. Saying no is good for others too – how else are they supposed to know your boundaries?

6. SAY YES. To things you love to do, to new experiences, to new opportunities, to things you actually want to do. Life is to be enjoyed, not endured.

SATURDAY 17

You are worthy of love

SUNDAY 18

Be your own unsinkable ship

November

MONDAY 19

Treat yourself to some delicious pampering

TUESDAY 20

Try out a new look

WEDNESDAY 21

It's ok to change your mind

Character cannot be developed in ease and quiet. Only through experience of trial and suffering can the soul be strengthened, ambition inspired, and success achieved.

It is not what we get, but who we become and what we contribute that gives meaning to our lives

Anthony Robbins

The duty of comedy is to correct men by amusing them.

Moliere

THURSDAY 22

Your health is your wealth – guard it

FRIDAY 23

Be kind to everyone – including yourself

SATURDAY 24

You cannot live other peoples' lives for them

SUNDAY 25

See beauty in unexpected places

Do the hard jobs first. The easy jobs will take care of themselves.

Dale Carnegie

November

MONDAY 26

Do something special for a dear friend

TUESDAY 27

Keep in touch with your friends

WEDNESDAY 28

Eat better, feel better

THURSDAY 29

Time is the most precious gift you have – value it, don't waste it

FRIDAY 30

Doubt kills more dreams than failure ever will – keep the faith

CHRISTMAS SHOPPING LIST

1. Buy a 2019 Get Up and Go Diary for all my friends.

2. Buy a Get Up and Go Travel Journal and plan my next trip.

BUCKET LIST FOR *December*

When you stop having dreams and ideals — well, you might as well stop altogether.

Marian Anderson

Never permit a dichotomy to rule your life, a dichotomy in which you hate what you do so you can have pleasure in your spare time. Look for a situation in which your work will give you as much happiness as your spare time.

Pablo Picasso

Although the world is full of suffering, it is full also of the overcoming of it.

You are the only person you can actually change.
— Katharine Hepburn

SATURDAY 1

Choose to see the world through grateful eyes

UNCONDITIONAL MOTHERLY LOVE

A mothers love is one of the most spiritual and primal of relationships. The act of beholding, of being taken in to our mothers arms – is one of the first sensations most of us experience in life. This union between mother and child unconsciously informs the infant of the pure goodness and worth of his or her being, of safety in the world, and of the great power in connection. By being held, we intrinsically understand that our presence in the world is appreciated and reciprocal, and that it is by the mutuality of a loving and supportive relationship that we transform and blossom.

SUNDAY 2

The future is created, not promised.

December

What people really need is love and mental healing. If we have the right mental attitude, our external circumstances will change for the better; then we'll have both a peaceful mind and a healthy body. Spirituality is the principle that teaches us to 'air condition' our minds. Trying to correct our external circumstances is like trying to air-condition the whole world; it cannot be done.

Amma

If you are not being treated with respect, check your price tag. Chances are you've marked yourself down. It's you who tells people what YOU are worth, by what you accept. Get off the clearance rack and get behind the glass where they keep all the valuables. You are WORTH it!

MONDAY 3

Look beyond your personal concerns

TUESDAY 4

Refuse to accept your own excuses

WEDNESDAY 5

Comparing your life with others is a recipe for upset

Walking with a friend in the dark is better than walking alone in the light.

THURSDAY 6

Be fully engaged in what you are doing today

FRIDAY 7

For maximum enjoyment have minimum expectation

SATURDAY 8

Celebrate everything you can

SUNDAY 9

Connect with nature – it will keep you grounded

I prefer a pleasant vice to an annoying virtue.
Moliere

You have been criticising yourself for years and it hasn't worked. Try approving of yourself and see what happens.
Louise L Hay

December

A little boy asked his mother, "why are you crying?"
"Because I'm a woman", she told him.
"I don't understand", he said.
His mum just hugged him and said, "and you never will".
Later the little boy asked his father, "why does mother seem to cry for no reason?"
"All women cry for no reason", was all his dad could say.
The little boy grew up and became a man, still wondering why women cry. Finally, he put in a call to God. When God answered, he asked "God, why do women cry so easily"?
God said: "When I made the woman she had to be special. I made her shoulders strong enough to carry the weight of the world, yet gentle enough to give comfort. I gave her an inner strength to endure childbirth and the rejection that many times comes from her children. I gave her a resilience that allows her to keep going when everyone else gives up, to take care of her family through sickness and fatigue without complaining. I gave her the sensitivity to love her children unconditionally, even when it seems like they have hurt her. I gave her strength to carry her husband through his faults and I gave her the wisdom to know that a good husband never hurts his wife, but sometimes tests her strengths and her resolve to stand beside him unfalteringly. And finally, I gave her a tear to shed. This is hers exclusively to use whenever it is needed.
"You see, my son", said God "the beauty of a woman is not in the clothes she wears, the figure that she carries, or the way she combs her hair. The beauty of a woman must be seen in her eyes, because that is the doorway to her heart – the place where love resides".

MONDAY **10**

Be happy that you do things differently

TUESDAY **11**

Congratulate yourself on all your accomplishments

> Age is something that doesn't matter, unless you are a cheese.
> *Luis Bunuel*

> *No man has a good enough memory to be a successful liar.*
> *Abraham Lincoln*

WEDNESDAY **12**

Dance lightly with life

THURSDAY **13**

Do your best and be satisfied

December

Fruit and nut cake
FROM MAMA RAE

INGREDIENTS
600gm dried fruit
1 teaspoon cinnamon
¼ teaspoon nutmeg
3 tablespoons coconut oil
1 teaspoon vanilla
1 orange
50gram chopped walnuts
3 eggs
200gm almond meal

THE HOW-TO PART
Put the dried fruit into a bowl, mix in the cinnamon, nutmeg. Add the coconut oil and vanilla, then the juice and zest of the orange and chopped walnuts. Stir through. Mix in the eggs and almond meal. Pour into a 20cm round cake tin and bake on 150 degrees for 90 minutes.

MAMA RAE'S INSIDE SECRETS
Experiment with dried peaches, prunes, date and apricots. Rather than walnuts, almonds are nice as well. If you don't have an orange, use 1½ lemons or limes.

FRIDAY 14

Share your dreams with others

SATURDAY 15

Pay attention to the details while being aware of the bigger picture

SUNDAY 16

Contentment is a pearl of great value

> It's my rule never to lose my temper
> 'til it would be detrimental to keep it.
>
> *Sean O'Casey*

MONDAY 17

Follow your own inner compass

> **When one door of happiness closes, another opens; but often we look so long at the closed door that we do not see the one which has been opened for us.**

TUESDAY 18

Harsh words don't break bones but they can break hearts

WEDNESDAY 19

Be loving, lovable and loved

THURSDAY 20

Keep a gratitude journal

December

FRIDAY 21

Give yourself permission to rest and heal without guilt

How to pair your cheese and wine

- A smooth, fatty cheese may go very well with a simarily smooth, slightly oily wine.
- Sweet wine contrasts very well with a cheese with high acidity.
- White wines go better with many cheeses than reds
- Not all red wines match with cheese. The most recommended are the fruity, light red wines
- Dry, fresh red wines are ideally suited to soft cheeses (especially goat ones).
- A wine with good acidity may be complemented by very salty cheeses.
- Cheeses can also be matched with beer or ciders.
- Try regional combinations (if possible), where the cheese and wine are from the same region.

SATURDAY 22

Keep searching and the answers will come

SUNDAY 23

Stay calm and relaxed no matter what

Common sense is the collection of prejudices acquired by age 18.
Albert Einstein

MONDAY 24

Write down what you love about your life

Stress less.
Dance it out.
Go for a walk.
Talk it over.
Go to bed early.
Ask for a hug.
Be grateful for what you have.
Look for solutions.
Plan a day out with friends.
Focus on what you can do.
Be the victor not the victim.

Pomegranate cosmo

MAKES 4

INGREDIENTS
2/3 cup of pomegranate juice
1/2 cup of vodka
1/4 cup of Grand Marnier or Cointreau
2 teaspoons of fresh lime juice
Ice
Lime slices

DIRECTIONS
1. Mix everything except the lime slices together.
2. Strain into a glass.
3. Garnish with a lime slice.

No one can make you feel inferior without your consent.
Eleanor Roosevelt

December

CHRISTMAS!!!

What a miraculous year. I wish everyone a beautiful holiday. It's not necessarily a joyous time for all... please have compassion for what people are dealing with. It takes nothing to be righteous and small when others aren't great with you. Be great with people because that is what honors you and serves them.

TUESDAY 25
Christmas Day

Merry Christmas!

WEDNESDAY 26

Participate in a fun activity – just for fun

THURSDAY 27

Believe in yourself and your abilities

*Listen to the mustn'ts, child
Listen to the don'ts.
Listen to
The shouldn'ts,
The impossibles,
The won'ts.
Listen to the never haves,
Then listen close to me.
Anything can happen child –
Anything can be.*

Shel Silverstein

FRIDAY 28

Acknowledge your personal best

SATURDAY 29

Be an inspiration to those around you

SUNDAY 30

Accept who you are without judgement or criticism

December

May you recognise in your life the presence, power, and light of your soul. May you realise that you are never alone, that your soul in its brightness and belonging connects you intimately with the rhythm of the universe.
May you have respect for you own individuality and difference. May you realise that the shape of your soul is unique, that you have a special destiny here, that behind the facade of your life there is something beautiful, good, and eternal happening. May you learn to see yourself with the same delight, pride, and expectation with which God sees you in every moment.

        John O'Donohue

MONDAY 31

Keep a journal for the coming year

Face your deficiencies and acknowledge them; but do not let them master you. Let them teach you patience, sweetness, insight.

DESIDERATA

Go placidly amid the noise and haste, and remember what peace there may be in silence. As far as possible without surrender be on good terms with all persons. Speak your truth quietly and clearly, and listen to others, even the dull and ignorant; they too have their story.

Avoid loud and aggressive persons, they are vexations to the spirit. If you compare yourself with others, you may become vain and bitter; for always there will be greater and lesser persons than yourself. Enjoy your achievements as well as your plans. Keep interested in your own career, however humble; it is a real possession in the changing fortunes of time. Exercise caution in your business affairs; for the world is full of trickery. But let this not blind you to what virtue there is; many persons strive for high ideals; and everywhere life is full of heroism.

Be yourself. Especially, do not feign affection. Neither be cynical about love; for in the face of all aridity and disenchantment it is perennial as the grass. Take kindly the counsel of the years, gracefully surrendering the things of youth. Nurture strength of spirit to shield you in sudden misfortune. But do not distress yourself with imaginings. Many fears are born of fatigue and loneliness. Beyond a wholesome discipline, be gentle with yourself.

You are a child of the universe, no less than the trees and the stars; you have a right to be here. And whether or not it is clear to you, no doubt the universe is unfolding as it should. Therefore be at peace with God, whatever you conceive him to be; and whatever your labours and aspirations, in the noisy confusion of life keep peace with your soul. With all its sham, drudgery and broken dreams, it is still a beautiful world. Be cheerful. Strive to be happy.

Max Ehrmann

2019 CALENDAR

JANAURY

Mo	Tu	We	Th	Fr	Sa	Su
	1	2	3	4	5	6
7	8	9	10	11	12	13
14	15	16	17	18	19	20
21	22	23	24	25	26	27
28	29	30	31			

FEBRUARY

Mo	Tu	We	Th	Fr	Sa	Su
				1	2	3
4	5	6	7	8	9	10
11	12	13	14	15	16	17
18	19	20	21	22	23	24
25	26	27	28			

MARCH

Mo	Tu	We	Th	Fr	Sa	Su
				1	2	3
4	5	6	7	8	9	10
11	12	13	14	15	16	17
18	19	20	21	22	23	24
25	26	27	28	29	30	31

APRIL

Mo	Tu	We	Th	Fr	Sa	Su
1	2	3	4	5	6	7
8	9	10	11	12	13	14
15	16	17	18	19	20	21
22	23	24	25	26	27	28
29	30					

MAY

Mo	Tu	We	Th	Fr	Sa	Su
		1	2	3	4	5
6	7	8	9	10	11	12
13	14	15	16	17	18	19
20	21	22	23	24	25	26
27	28	29	30	31		

JUNE

Mo	Tu	We	Th	Fr	Sa	Su
					1	2
3	4	5	6	7	8	9
10	11	12	13	14	15	16
17	18	19	20	21	22	23
24	25	26	27	28	29	30

JULY

Mo	Tu	We	Th	Fr	Sa	Su
1	2	3	4	5	6	7
8	9	10	11	12	13	14
15	16	17	18	19	20	21
22	23	24	25	26	27	28
29	30	31				

AUGUST

Mo	Tu	We	Th	Fr	Sa	Su
			1	2	3	4
5	6	7	8	9	10	11
12	13	14	15	16	17	18
19	20	21	22	23	24	25
26	27	28	29	30	31	

SEPTEMBER

Mo	Tu	We	Th	Fr	Sa	Su
						1
2	3	4	5	6	7	8
9	10	11	12	13	14	15
16	17	18	19	20	21	22
23	24	25	26	27	28	29
30						

OCTOBER

Mo	Tu	We	Th	Fr	Sa	Su
	1	2	3	4	5	6
7	8	9	10	11	12	13
14	15	16	17	18	19	20
21	22	23	24	25	26	27
28	29	30	31			

NOVEMBER

Mo	Tu	We	Th	Fr	Sa	Su
				1	2	3
4	5	6	7	8	9	10
11	12	13	14	15	16	17
18	19	20	21	22	23	24
25	26	27	28	29	30	

DECEMBER

Mo	Tu	We	Th	Fr	Sa	Su
						1
2	3	4	5	6	7	8
9	10	11	12	13	14	15
16	17	18	19	20	21	22
23	24	25	26	27	28	29
30	31					

INTRODUCING OUR LATEST PUBLICATION

Get Up and Go Heroes

These 24 real-life stories from Get Up and Go Publications Ltd shed a revealing light on how people overcome extraordinary challenges and keep going even when nothing seems to be working.

From extraordinary and moving situations, to moments and decisions that change the trajectory of a life, the pieces in this book give revealing insights into how to overcame difficulty. Some experiences are a gift and others a lesson. At times the lesson simply is that apparent failure is the universe's way of nudging you to make changes.

Many of us believe that we need to be extraordinary to achieve great things, but, as this book shows, heroes are ordinary people 'given being and action by something bigger than themselves'.

The book was launched at the 2017 Get Up and Go event in Sligo, Ireland – Get Up and Go with Passion and Purpose.

The contributors have either been speakers at previous Get Up and Go Events, or potential speakers at future events, as they each have an inspirational message to share, with an intention to empower, motivate and encourage you, the reader, to 'get up and go' forward in your own life.

The annual Get Up and Go event is not for profit and all proceeds from Get Up and Go Heroes will be donated to Cystic Fibrosis Ireland, Pieta House, Northwest Simon and CHAB School Cambodia.

Copies of Heroes can be purchased on
www.getupadgodiary.com

Follow us on our Facebook page Get Up and Go Events for details of future events.

FOR MORE COPIES VISIT OUR WEBSITE
www.getupandgodiary.com

OR CONTACT US ON
info@getupandgodiary.com

Postal address: **Get Up and Go Publications Ltd, Camboline, Hazelwood, Sligo, Ireland F91 NP04**.

DIRECT ORDER FORM (please complete by ticking boxes)

PLEASE SEND ME:

- The Irish Get Up and Go Diary **2018** ☐ **2019** ☐ €10/£9   Quantity ☐
- The Irish Get Up and Go Diary (case bound) **2018** ☐ **2019** ☐ €15/£13   Quantity ☐
- Get Up and Go Diary for Busy Women **2018** ☐ **2019** ☐ €10/£9   Quantity ☐
- Get Up and Go Diary for Busy Women (case bound) **2018** ☐ **2019** ☐ €15/£13   Quantity ☐
- Get Up and Go Diary **2018** ☐ **2019** ☐ €10/£9   Quantity ☐
- Get Up and Go Diary for Girls **2018** ☐ **2019** ☐ €10/£9   Quantity ☐
- Get Up and Go Diary for Boys **2018** ☐ **2019** ☐ €10/£9   Quantity ☐
- Get Up and Go Travel Journal ☐ €12/£10.50   Quantity ☐
- Get Up and Go Genius Journal ☐ €15/£13   Quantity ☐
- Get Up and Go Student Journal (homework journal) ☐ €14/£12   Quantity ☐
- Get Up and Go Heroes (all proceeds to charity) ☐ €10/£9   Quantity ☐
- The Confidence to Succeed (by Donna Kennedy) ☐ €12.50/£10   Quantity ☐

Total number of copies ☐

P+P WITHIN IRELAND €2.50 PER COPY.
P+P INTERNATIONAL/OVERSEAS €3.50 PER COPY.

I enclose cheque/postal order for (total amount including P+P): _____

Name: _____

Address: _____
_____

Contact phone number: _____ Email: _____

For orders over eight items, please contact us on 086 1788631 / 071 9146717